Walking With My Foot In My Mouth

Patricia Finn

R.D. Davis Publishing
Sarasota, Florida

Walking with My Foot in My Mouth

Copyright © 2020 Patricia Finn

All rights reserved. No portion of this book may be reproduced mechanically, electronically, or by any other means, including photocopying, without written permission from the publisher. It is illegal to copy this book, post it to a website, or distribute it by any other means without permission from the publisher.

Published by R.D. Davis Publishing
Sarasota, Florida

Designed by Joe Eckstein, Imagine! Studios
www.ArtsImagine.com

ISBN: 978-0-578-66122-3 (paperback)
ISBN: 978-0-578-68862-6 (e-book)

Library of Congress Control Number: 2020936992

Sixth R.D. Davis Publishing printing: July 2025

Contents

Miss Adventure / 1

Dental Danger
The Front Passenger Seat
Ballet Blues
Go Gators
Busted
Caution — Vultures Crossing
How Was Your Weekend?
Witch Laundromat?
Silence Is Golden
My Friend Gym
Supermarket Sabotage
Low Tech Alert
The Repair Nightmare

To the Past and Beyond / 39

The Times They Are A Changin' — Bob Who?
Born Blonde
Two Cans And A String
Lock-Lock

Order in the Classroom
Don't Smile—Say "Cheese"
Wedding Bells

Hi-Ho Hi-Ho / 59

Dear Reader
Fifty Hour a Week Toys
Dare to Decorate
The DMV and Me
Coffee—Office Style
In Keeping With Love And Marriage
Raccoon Rukus

Opinionated Opinions / 85

Weather or Not Here I Come
Thank You for the Lovely Plant
Please Pass the Dressing
Big Bad Kids
Ahh Micanopy!
The Cost of Living, or Not
Uh-Oh Here Come the Dolls
What's Gat You're Chewing?
Once Upon a Time
April Showers Bring

The Right to Bare Arms
Treat Or Treat
The Lone Ranger
Roses Are Red — Violets Are Black
Yummy Art

Word for Word / 129

What's Happening to Words?
The Mom
Write or Wrong?
Babble Works
Bumper Sticker Readings $5.00
Feel the Beat
Proverbial Wisdom
Different Strokes for Different Folks
Oops
And the Winning Name Is . . .
Please, Honk and Thank You
Is This News Fit to Print?
Yummy Catfish

Tasty Very Tasty / 167

Raising the Coffee Bar
Thank You, Johnny Appleseed

Cupcake Wars
Cornbread Angel
A Piece of Cake
Guilty as Charged
Le Petit Dejeuner
So Real
Roses Are Red
Still Talking Turkey

LIFE, LIBERTY, AND THE PURSUIT OF HAPPINESS / 195

A Thrifty Addiction
Warm Fish
M & M
Probably Not
Successful Failure
Mommy Get Your Gun
Say Goodnight, Gracie
Sole Analysis
Late Bloomer — Baby Boomer

About the Author / 227

MISS ADVENTURE

Dental Danger

Now that I have crossed the sixty-year threshold, it is important to take care of my teeth. I floss. I brush. I gargle. I don't want to skip any step that might result in the dreaded tooth loss. Recently, I spent three hours in a dental chair. This gave me time to think. I thought about my new diet plan; I thought about past dental experiences. I thought about the posh dentist I went to in Arizona. It is all coming back in HD mental meandering.

Throughout the office, this dentist had expensive wood paneling on the ceiling. Every patient had their own large screen TV in front of a comfy leather chair. He also had an assistant who started to prep the wrong side of my mouth. I said, "I think the Doctor is working on the right." Dr. K, feeling financially secure enough to have a cavalier attitude while drilling, liked to sing to his staff. They in turn would sing back a reply. It was sort of a Swiss yodeling with a disco beat. Afterward, I told my daughter, "The dentist was singing to his staff, where do they do that?" Her reply, "Scottsdale."

Recently, I spent three hours in a dental chair. This gave me time to think.

Is Scottsdale the only place where someone can have a dental experience that will make their molars rattle? No. In Florida I went to a dentist who had a collection of dental signs in the waiting area. A realistic hobby for a dentist except these signs all had lights and movement. Smiles began and faded, lights were flashing everywhere, it was sort of a dental arcade experience. Even at the reception desk, there was a moving miniature dentist brushing. "This is very different," I said handing my new patient forms to the woman sentenced to work there. Expressionless and without looking up she said, "The doctor likes it." I thought longingly of the mild mannered, military trained dentist who had treated my family for over twenty years. He retired. What a great dentist. He retired the year I divorced. An important caring man was gone from my life.

While searching for a replacement, I had the nerve to ask one dentist not to give me X-rays. He told me to leave and threatened to call the police. "Leave now or I will call the police." I attract this type of person. I wasn't loud, rude or demanding. I simply said, "Please, no X-rays." Dentists like to tell us that we get less harmful radiation from X-rays than from sunlight. They overlook the fact that my skin was made for sunlight and the inside of my mouth was not.

Back to Scottsdale. I am head down, feet up, dentist on the right, assistant on the left. Something is placed on my chest. Dentist to assistant, "Do not rest tools on the patient, she is not a table." Slightly offended by the slur to the shape of my chest, I tense. A professional choice, the assistant does it again. Again, the dentist says, "Do not rest tools on the patient." I want to sit up and say, "Didn't you hear Dr. K? He said not to rest tools on the patient." The process is finished, and the dentist leaves the room. He directs his assistant to do something inside my mouth. As soon as he leaves the room, she puts a tool on my chest. Defiant teenage behavior at best. Do I complain? Do I tell Dr. K., "Your assistant disobeyed you."? Saying nothing, I paid my bill and left. Why? Dental X-rays must have done something to my brain.

The Front Passenger Seat

I enjoy meeting friends for a midday cup of coffee. I recently met my friend Barb for an afternoon coffee chit-chat. She was late. When she came rushing into the café, she breathlessly explained that she had been driven to meet me by her son. She had ridden in the front passenger seat. "Water, just water, please. Oh, thank you."

The front passenger seat is a challenging place. Once strapped in, you are at the mercy of the driver. For any mom, riding in the passenger seat of a car driven by one of your children is a challenge. I have taken death defying rides and unfortunately in my case, my credibility is low. What does that mean? My opinion as a passenger is easily dismissed with, "How many accidents have you had, Mom?" How many accidents have I had? The fact that I have been driving four to five times longer is not taken into account. I am silenced. Closing my eyes is the answer and I sit thinking what a wonderful thing it is to have eye lids. Are we racing down the interstate, insanely fast, passing cars on the right, on the left, then swerving into place—too close behind a big truck? How would I know? My eyes are closed.

Riding with my daughter is riding with a multi-tasker. When I am a passenger and my daughter is driving, a phone is added to the experience. She is talking on the phone and steering with one finger of her left hand. I close my eyes and grip the seat. How did this happen? This is my car. My mind goes back to a ride home from a church social with a friend's granddaughter at the wheel. I was sitting next to Nola. Her seat was pushed back as far as possible, she was reclining parallel to the floor, steering with her knees, and eating fried chicken from a box balanced on her tummy. Nola is way over the speed limit; she has a disposition not to be challenged and she hates me. Gripping my seat, I close my eyes.

Have you ever ridden in the passenger seat of a car driven by someone who finds fault with and is angry at all the idiot drivers? Not to be sexist, in this case scenario the driver is usually a man. The innocent passenger is forced to listen to what is wrong with the idiots. Do you dare suggest that the idiots can't hear the insults or the critique of their driving? No, because listening to the driver rant is part of being in the passenger seat. Not that I have ever gotten out of a car at a Stop sign and preferred to walk home.

Do your own driving. Don't be the passenger.

What is the answer to all of this? Do your own driving. Don't be the passenger. In case you don't have a list, I will share my list of convenient excuses to use when you hear, "Get in, I'll drive."

1. "Oh. Thank you,
   but I need to take my own car because I need to see if the store is still open and I might have to stop and get something very important, and I might have to leave early, and I need to leave early and stop at the store."

2. "Sorry but I can't ride with you, I will take my own car because if I ride with you, I will die."

3. "Gee, thanks but I'll drive, I have to clear my head and a high-speed adrenalin rush works every time. You're welcome to ride with me."

Ballet Blues

I went to the ballet last weekend. I enjoyed it. I give the company a lot of credit for entertaining several hundred people for over two hours without uttering a word. Ballet now includes props and costumes. Traditional ballet must have left the stage when I wasn't watching and has been replaced with dance theater that left me spell bound, to use an equally dramatic phrase.

The performance was wonderful, but I had trouble enjoying myself because I am afraid of heights. I had two ticket choices. I could sit in the orchestra and pay $100.00 or purchase a seat in the Balcony for $50.00. I picked the balcony and was air-lifted to my seat. I did not realize that 'balcony' was another word for ceiling. I was so high up that I was afraid to look around. For twenty minutes, I assured myself that when the house lights go down, I will be able to focus on the stage and forget that my head is touching the ceiling, and my nose is starting to bleed. I was frozen with fear because I was higher than the lights and the other technical

> *The performance was wonderful, but I had trouble enjoying myself because I am afraid of heights.*

looking things that were suspended from the ceiling. Should I leave? I couldn't. The aisle was so tight that my knees were touching my chin and the only escape was if half of the row (I was in the middle) stood and shimmied out first.

Ninety percent of the audience was over the age of seventy. Who will be watching in twenty years? The woman next to me was wearing my mother's mink wrap. "Wait a minute Miss Pat, it is time to stop complaining, to stop thinking about how many months went into a production that will last two hours, and didn't someone once say, "Critical minds can't enjoy"?

Go Gators

Disastrous restaurant experiences may be a dime a dozen but mine is a little different. The service was terrible, but the decision to leave was not because we waited a mere hour for our food. We left because I had an encounter with something that strikes fear into my very soul, a description which demonstrates why I write a humor column and not adventure stories.

My son was visiting from New York and for lunch we spontaneously chose an Asian restaurant with a beautiful lake view. I asked to sit outside, and we moved our table from the deck to a grassy bank to be even closer to the water. Then, terror struck. (I am getting better at this.) My son said, "Oh. Look at the young alligator swimming to the bank. People must throw food to him from the deck. He is just a teenager." Then, I said, "I hate alligators." Big mistake. According to my son's theory, my negative comment was intuitively understood by the young gator. Next, I look teen gator in the eye and again say, "I hate you." My son responds with, "Mom, don't do that." The rest is sort of a blur but somewhere in the timeline that followed, I challenge the gator, my son comments on my negative vibe and the monster gets out of the water and starts up the bank. Have you ever seen me move really fast? Carrying a pot of tea?

I was past the deck and inside before you could say, "Here comes the gator."

Florida has beautiful lakes, but they all go to waste because they are filled to the brim with man eating, carnivorous alligators. So sad, if we were in the North, says this Yankee transplant, there is no swimming like lake swimming. I live near Payne's Prairie. This prairie once was a lake. It is now filled with alligators meandering in their clumsy menacing way from water puddle to water puddle. I am told that the prairie has wild horses, but I have never stayed long enough to see any. Have I ever eaten gator? When people eat alligator, they compare it with chicken. No, I have never eaten gator, or possum, or snake. I know, I am picky, picky. Because people don't raise alligators for food, they must be caught in the wild. Driving behind a slow-moving pickup truck in a Florida resort town, I wondered, "What's in the back of that truck?" It looked like a pile of old tires. It was a dead gator. Ooh nasty. Not as nasty as watching the pickup drive to the back of a popular seafood restaurant.

My hatred of alligators is a little tricky because

> *Florida has beautiful lakes, but they all go to waste because they are filled to the brim with man eating, carnivorous alligators.*

I lived in a Florida college town that is the unofficial Alligator Capitol of the World. The University of Florida proudly refers to itself as The Gator Nation. All University of Florida graduates from the dawn of civilization to the end of time are members in The Gator Nation. Their school loyalty exceeds extreme patriotism. Gator images abound. My peers, the past grads who are now in their 60's and 70's happily wear Gator caps and drink coffee from Gator mugs. Gatorade anyone? Do I conform? Of course, I conform. Everyone who knows me knows that I am weak and easily influenced. My conformity is best seen at football games when I loudly join the chant, "Go Gators."

Busted

In a small town you can get away with behavior that would never be accepted in a city. When I told a friend about the bus experiences I had in a small Florida town, she said that in New York City, the passengers would not have let the bus drivers do that. That is not exactly what she said, but I omit all references to physical violence.

Once upon a time, I was using the local bus for transportation. I had experienced a car accident and was planning to give myself a rest before getting back on the road. If this sounds like a fairy tale—it is. The reality of having destroyed a car that I couldn't afford to replace is not something to put in print. The fact that I had waved goodbye to my underinsured vehicle from the other side of a junkyard fence is sad, sad, sad.

Always an optimist, I welcomed the opportunity to relax and not drive. I did not consider that this relaxation would include waiting on the bus while the driver ran into McDonalds to pick up his breakfast

> *In a small town you can get away with behavior that would never be accepted in a city.*

which he thoughtfully chose to bring back in a little bag, and not eat inside. The first time this happened, I looked around in confusion hoping that the other passengers might share my disbelief and offer some support to my conclusion that this is not appropriate bus driver behavior. My teacher training has taught me to use terms like, 'inappropriate behavior' as opposed to, "What are you doing? Are you crazy?" The other passengers sat patiently, and if they saw my expression of disbelief they looked away, mildly embarrassed. I was the newcomer; they had been putting up with this for years and after all, he *is* the bus driver.

The next scenario is not just inappropriate bus driver behavior but, "We're calling your parents and you're going home," bus driver behavior. The stop before mine was in front of a chain supermarket. There were only two passengers with me on the bus, two Asian men who were happily chatting in Chinese. Perhaps they were new to this country and, being newcomers, they may have thought that what we were about to witness was normal.

The bus stopped in front of a supermarket parking lot. A third Asian man pushed his cart out of the parking lot and down the driveway that connected the parking lot with the road. He basically had the audacity to leave his grocery cart pushed neatly against the curb out of the way of cars. He stepped innocently onto the bus, showed the bus driver his pass and sat down. The driver flew into a rage. She stood up, pointed to the cart, and screaming, she ordered the man off the bus and commanded him to move his cart back into the parking lot. I couldn't believe my ears. The man, abashed by her outburst and fearing I don't know what, dutifully left the bus, and moved his cart.

Shamed with thoughts of, "What would Rosa Parks have done?" I took it all in speechlessly. I didn't want to engage this bus driver, she's big, loud, mean and crazy. The three men started conversing in Chinese and well, they didn't seem upset. I guess by fascist standards this was not a major issue. The next stop was mine. I hopped off the bus and nodded to the driver, "Have a nice day." I was thinking—if I hurry, hurry, hurry I can get to the car dealership and be driving by tomorrow.

Caution—Vultures Crossing

Our public park system is wonderful and one of my favorite destinations is the local State Park. For $15 I can rent a bike and pedal through endless acres of pristine wilderness. I occasionally spot a deer and deliberately avoid the alligators. No reptile is going to spoil my day in nature. Unfortunately, alligators abound because I am in Florida and well, . . . it is swampy. The Park has a paddle boat ride on a small lake but because of the you-know-what, I decline. The water excursion is aboard a vessel called The Gator Gal which is more than enough to finalize my decision not to come on board.

I occasionally spot a deer and deliberately avoid the alligators.

As I leisurely bike along, I am reminded of the vast expanses of untouched land in Arizona and the occasional sign along a lonely road, CAUTION WILD HORSES. Parks do a wonderful job of alerting us to wildlife and what visitor to Yellowstone is surprised to see the famous DON'T FEED THE BEARS signs. (Who would feed a bear?) But . . . Wait! What's this! WARNING—VULTURES MAY CAUSE DAMAGE TO VEHICLES. What? Vultures? Damage?

Those big birds that I see everywhere are *vultures*? Where am I? Hell? "Get a grip, Miss Pat, enjoy the trees, the vast expanse of pristine land unhindered by man's overreaching encroachment into God's creation. Calm down, take a deep breath. Recite a calming poem. Maybe the vultures eat dead alligators. Now, is that better?—Where'd she go?"

How Was Your Weekend?

"How was your weekend?" Me? My weekend? Pretty exciting. I took the cats to Long John Silver for lunch. They love it. Brinie had the cod sandwich. Simon likes the tuna. We always sit in a booth by the window so they can look out. Other than that, nothing much. I walked to the post office and mailed a letter. I vacuumed. I even emptied the vacuum cleaner bag which is a big event. "Miss Pat, don't you ever get bored?" Bored? No. Not at all. I peeled potatoes, took a nap, robbed a bank and went grocery shopping. Same old, same old. I like to limit what I do on the weekend. Sometimes I will go out for a cup of coffee or walk next door for an ice cream.

On Friday, I got a call from a close friend. This weekend they are going to Pennsylvania, then to New Jersey and then back to New York. Their list of activities will exceed my annual To Do list. I can't relate because I enjoy doing nothing. In fact, I have perfected it. How did I perfect doing nothing? Very thoughtfully. On any given weekend, I might (gulp) vacuum. Then rest. Write a little. Rest. Pet the cats. Rest. Walk across the room. Rest. This weekend was unusual I did go out. You can't be a homebody forever; got to keep the mind active, see the world, have adventures.

After taking the cats to lunch, I went to a Thrift Shop and spent $20 on stuff I will never use. The prices were so great! They even had an armoire on sale for $49 plus an extra 30% off if you pick it up in three days. I eyed a tea pot shaped like a pumpkin but why be extravagant?

My weekends are full, full, full to the brim and over-flowing, flowing, flowing onto the floor, down the stairs and into the street. What a mess. Living in a small town like Micanopy, they had to call the police. Not to be disrespectful of the police because I am respectful and grateful but, in this town they don't have a lot to do. One day, I saw three police cars parked by a pick-up truck which was obviously under suspicion. "Oooh. What could it be?" When I walked back again, the police were gone, and I got to see for myself. There were two dead turkeys in the back of the truck. They were loosely covered with burlap. Dead turkeys? Three squad cars? Crime city.

My weekends are full, full, full to the brim and over-flowing, flowing, flowing onto the floor, down the stairs and into the street.

In today's world it is all about using the right words: handicapped vs crippled, financially challenged vs broke, mentally challenged vs nuts. We are very kind and careful when we label people and personal attributes. We politely say that people 'pass away.' They stopped dropping dead about ten years ago. I have considered that I may be lazy. This is possible. So, with political correctness in mind, I am not lazy or boring. I am home oriented.

Witch Laundromat?

I love visiting my adult children and when I do, I help with the chores. Last week, I was cursed by a witch while doing my son's laundry. "That could only happen to you, Dobro," My son said. He is a mature adult and chooses to no longer call me Mom. Instead, he calls me Dobro. A Dobro is a musical instrument like a dulcimer. At this point in my life, I don't care. Dodo (like the bird) would not be okay.

So, here is sweet Dobro at the laundromat, sorting and waiting—such a good mom. I will not divulge the exact location; but it was a typical open-air laundromat in the state of Florida. Clothes are in and I sat on a folding chair facing the street. A woman strolling with a sun umbrella, stopped, looked and approached me saying, "Well, look at you sitting here so pretty and nice, I will now put a curse on you."

I am not known for my quick responses, and I was taken off guard. She proceeded to hold both of my hands while standing in front of me, her back to the traffic. This is important because I had trouble hearing what she was saying, and unlike the average American approached by a witch, I sat there and considered what to do. I could have said, "Be gone, Evil One," or "Help". When she finished, I mumbled, "You can't curse me." I have a certain amount of confidence in that area. She cackled and flew away.

Shortly after my encounter at the laundromat, I had another unconventional experience, this time it was at the public library. I found some interesting books and sat at a table with a nice window view. The room was full of empty tables and low and behold who should decide to sit across from me but a middle-aged man from Saturn who owned 200 bicycles. I am not stupid, if you are from Saturn how did you get a library card? Inside I am screaming, "Leave me alone. Go away. Sit by someone else." Or because I am polite, I could have said, "Excuse me while I take my interesting, unfinished reading somewhere else. I don't suppose you would consider moving?" Saying nothing, I left.

When I passed the library bike rack, I saw that my Saturn friend had come on one of his 200 bikes. It had a stuffed hobby horse head attached to the handle-bars. Walking home, I decided that it is because I allow my son to call me Dobro that I have these frequent strange encounters. If I insisted on being called 'mom' or the antiquated term 'mother,' none of this would happen.

When she finished, I mumbled, "You can't curse me."

Silence Is Golden

I love the internet. It is wonderful to be so easily connected to people everywhere. We are just a click away from housewives in Denmark, bankers in London, terrorists in Nigeria. We truly have access to a global marketplace.

"So, why the long face, Miss Pat? Did something go wrong? Tell me about it. What happened?"

"Well, I was so happy and excited and then so disappointed."

"Go on, I am listening."

I am counseling myself. Counseling myself because after my internet experience, I am the only person I trust.

"I was planning to move back to Florida (sniffle) and, and . . ."

"There, there, take your time."

"I looked online for a house to rent and found one. My dream house, small but stylish. It was on the bay, in a good neighborhood, and the price was so right."

"And?"

"I communicated for weeks online with the owners, a missionary couple in Africa. I even had

After my internet experience, I am the only person I trust.

a friend visit the address to make sure everything looked to be on the up and up. I was, (sob) in love with a house."

Using my most controlled and responsible voice, I inquire of myself:

"And did you move into your dream house?"

"No, blankety-blank. I didn't."

"And why not, Alice?"

"They deceived me and told me to use Western Union and send a deposit to an African address.

"Did you send the money, my dear?"

"No, I was stopped in time by family and friends. A friend found the real owners. The real owners had rented out the house six months earlier at twice the price. They had advertised it on the internet."

Enough counseling. Readers, beware. When I shared my Nigerian email correspondence with my son his response was, "How could you have believed a word of this?" "Well, I was suspicious when they said a cousin was going to use the house for a few weeks becau go to waste se they had told me that it was unfurnished."

I wish I could say, "Lesson learned." Others, like me (maybe there is *one* other like me?) just don't get the scam part of being connected. Today, the crooks are from far away, but just as crafty. Crafty? Like selling fine crafted copper coffee sets on the internet? I'm in trouble now. I will confess to Rip Off Scenario #2. No counseling was needed this time. This was very scary, and if my children read this, they may take away my password. I was looking through old emails for a poem, and I saw the words: Big Silent. "Why the Big Silent?" Who talks like that? We say in the President's English, "Why haven't I heard from you?" or "Why have you been so silent?" Who puts together an awkward phrase like, "Why the Big Silent?" I'll tell you who, the same ones that sent me a check for $2000 priority mail and told me to deposit it and send them $500. How does this happen?

I advertised a copper coffee set on the internet and got an immediate response. My buyer was a little odd but she assured me that I would receive a check priority mail and someone would come to pick up 'the item.' You can imagine my surprise when I opened the envelope and saw my generous tip. The check was for $2000! Who says crime doesn't pay? I was instructed to just make the deposit and send them money. Very confusing. Why was I sending money when I was the 'seller'? With trembling hands, I tore up the check and never answered the emails wanting to know: "Why the Big Silent?"

My Friend Gym

I have joined a gym. This is not the first time. I am very good at joining. I would say it is about my fifth or sixth gym experience. It is not that I would rather sit and watch TV eating rum raisin ice cream, nope, not me. I am all about working out and being healthy. I am also abandoning negative thoughts like, "What's happening that we sit at a desk all day then go and work out to stay fit?" I love the gym. I did not join a cool gym, a fancy gym or expensive gym. I joined a Jr. College gym. Who works out at a Jr. College gym? Young men with big muscles. They are body minded and serious about their big muscles. I try to understand the mind-set, but I can't relate. I have never been body minded. I watch them and try to imagine what it would be like to walk around thinking that I had a great body. Completely foreign. My body is something I tolerate and live with; it's sort of like a sibling.

I will now shock readers who believe they can improve their bodies with exercise. I honestly don't know anyone who has

> *I watch them and try to imagine what it would be like to walk around thinking that I had a great body.*

done that. The people that I see at the gym look good and have always looked good. They are maintaining not recreating. It is true that I am arguing with myself. Shouldn't I try to reshape and lose weight? It's something to consider. Afterall, I have joined a gym.

Sometimes I get, "Why is *she* here?" looks but my fellow gym partners are focused on their own exercise routines. What does Miss Pat do at the Jr. College gym? They know I have arrived because all the pins go from 100+ pounds to the 10 lb. slot. Next, the seat comes up. I am considerate because I never stay more than two minutes on any one machine. The secret to my new gym success is the purchase of a way too expensive but very essential arm band phone holder and ear plugs. Thanks to Pandora, I have one hour of Southern Gospel pumped into my head and soul. Thanks to Pandora, I exercise with a smile and occasionally can be heard saying, "Glory" under my breath. I am enjoying my gym experience. I have more energy and feel great. I use every machine and it takes one hour. Work those arms, legs, back, and core. Push and puff and "Glory, glory, glory." When I get home, I reward myself. I've earned it, all that pulling and pushing. Now I can relax and watch TV. Will this be with or without ice cream?

Supermarket Sabotage

One happy day, two troubled youth targeted me at the supermarket. I was standing in front of a frozen food display when out of the corner of my detective eye, I noticed the young men staring at me and whispering. Hmmm, that's funny. I decided to wait and see what they were up to. Bad choice. The two heavily chained, leather clad and swastika tattooed young men were plotting to sabotage me. Yes, me. I later learned that 'troubled youth' i.e. skin heads, do this for fun, anything upside down or out of the ordinary such as crashing grocery carts into housewives was considered sport. Deliberately looking away, the two proceeded to walk toward me, and slammed their cart into mine. Then, whoosh—they were gone.

This catastrophic event happened more than twenty years ago, and I am now ready to declare with some pride, "Nobody messes with this mom." When I regained my composure, I did what any red-blooded American Mom would do. I went after them. Swiftly searching each aisle, I found my assailants by the large scale near the entrance of the store. I have often considered the function of this strategically placed scale, so conveniently giving us an opportunity to weigh ourselves before we go home and eat all the food we just bought.

I did what any red-blooded American Mom would do. I went after them.

As I approached them, I heard one say with great surprise, "It's that lady." I then proceeded to look the other way and rammed my cart into theirs. My husband was furious. "Why didn't you go to the manager?" he asked. "What were you thinking? Nobody does that. Are you crazy?" I was quickly told by concerned family members that my encounter occurred at a time when women were having their purses grabbed and being knocked down. I weighed 120 pounds (yes, it was decades ago) and stood a massive 5'4". I was the guest storyteller at the local library, the nice lady with the puppets.

With this incident in mind, I have developed a solution to the skin head problem. Remember the adage, 'Clothes make the man'? Well, clothes can unmake the bully. Anyone belonging to a hate group will have to wear suits and ties. They will no longer be allowed to dress tough. What would it be like if the tough people only wore soft pastel colors? No leather, no chains. The outside will not reflect the inside. What will this accomplish? I think it is an answer to crime in America today. Why hasn't someone thought of this sooner?

I never saw my attackers again. That evening, as the sun set over my kitchen sink, I sat tall in the saddle. Tell the manager? Never.

Low Tech Alert

I am phoneless. Last weekend my phone's annoying alerts were reduced to a guttural groan and then silence. Life has its stumbling blocks, call them bumps in the road. I will not resort to saying, "Blanketly, blank, blank, blank." Before giving me the silent treatment, I couldn't get my phone to stop talking to me, so I stuffed it in a drawer. Did I scream, "Shut up" before slamming the drawer? Not me, I would never do that. Retrieving my phone from a cocoon of sweaters, I pushed buttons to no avail. I tried sweetly coaxing, but nothing worked. It was time to go to the experts at the phone retail shop.

My phone is a budget phone. Because it is a budget phone, I cannot locate a store in a neighborhood I would refer to as friendly or safe. I need to drive eight miles away and into The Danger Zone. Fortunately, in this town the danger zone is not too dangerous, but it is out of my comfort zone. My comfort zone is a two-mile square adjacent to the snow-bird Amish neighborhood. The specialty is pies, not crime. Clutching my barely breathing phone, I drove north past Main Street and into the neighborhood where a friend's son was robbed. The assailant jumped into a dumpster to hide. Not thinking clearly, he poked his head up and waved.

The phone retail shop shares a strip mall with a pawn shop, a tattoo parlor and a small café with a sign that reads: EAT TO LIVE. LIVE TO RIDE. Motorcycles are everywhere. Driving up, "What's this?" Do I see someone pulling the shade and placing CLOSED on the door? But fellas it's *me*. Grammy. Remember me? Last week I needed all apps turned on, the week before I needed all apps turned off. Then I was back again for help activating a new phone.

A HELP WANTED sign is in the window. Help is wanted, not because they are busy but because no one wants to work there. The counter is set way in the back and the store is empty. The absence of customers is not surprising but there are also no products on display. I take the long, lonely walk from the front door to the counter. A woman is there. She tests my phone and declares it to be DOA.

I am not attached to my phone; I don't love it but I am living in the twenty-first century and bumbling along like a dummy because I am not giving technology the effort it deserves. I am busy. Will I replace my dead phone? The answer is "Yes." I will drive back to The Danger Zone to be set up with a new product that will enable me to connect with the world and be a twenty-first century grammy who can Skype, Zoom and watch podcasts.

I am not attached to my phone; I don't love it.

The Repair Nightmare

Not all parenting experiences are wonderful. Twenty plus years ago, I happily loaded my newly serviced vehicle with my daughter's boxes and proceeded to follow her from Florida's west coast to Miami to attend Art School, a common American scenario. The plan was to stay with her overnight and return the next day. Somewhere south of home, I turned off the highway into a gas station, and got out of my car to pump gas. I like pumping gas. It gives me a false sense of independence, freedom, and power. Unfortunately, this time was to be an exception because the pump didn't work. Silly me, the pump didn't work because the gas station was closed. I thought, "Not a problem, I'll just stop further down the road." My daughter was about thirty miles an hour ahead of me, and I was having fun. I did not know that the bottom was about to fall out of my engine and my life.

I got back into my car and turned the key. Dead. Nothing. Oh, something must be wrong. This incident happened before every American purse was blessed with a cell phone. Still smiling, I started to walk to find a phone. I smiled because I felt worldly and wise. A worldly and wise woman has road service. After three months of being single, I was on a first name basis with the AAA locksmith. I will now just state the facts. I walked for five miles in a raging blizzard. I found a phone booth next to the Stay Away Cafe and waited two hours for road service. After being towed forty-five minutes to my daughter's new address, the driver told me that they would not take a check to cover my extended towing charge because it was not written on a local bank. Instead, the towing company would impound my car. This was Saturday and I would have to wait until Monday to get it back. Could I pay cash? $200? Even I knew not to carry cash. This was getting very confusing. I experienced a chill and said goodbye to my car.

On Monday, my car was released from the towing center, and brought to a service station. I was told that the transmission was shot, and it would be five days before it could be fixed. They also said something that sounded like "No oil." There is a difference between rebuilding a transmission and having a transmission replaced. I know that. Rebuild. Repair. Replace. Replace is never the same thing as rebuild or repair. Rebuild is to build again, repair is to fix. Replace means another one, maybe new, maybe not. Rebuild. Repair. Replace. Rebuild. Repair. Replace. I found a luncheonette and ordered a latte.

As promised, on Friday, I welcomed back my precious car. I had nothing to pack so I eagerly said goodbye to my daughter who had been on a whirlwind of new student activities. She asked why I had worn the same dress for a week. Life has its ups and downs. I was glad to be back up. Smiling, I pulled into line at the toll booth leading to Home Sweet Home. As I tossed in my money, a gentle rain started. Then, something strange happened.

I watch a French language show on PBS which enables me to say with confidence "Quelle Bizarre!" My car stopped running. The engine was dead. I put my foot on the accelerator, and . . . nothing. It would not start. I was at a toll booth, and it was now pouring. I had just spent a week having the engine either rebuilt or replaced, and everyone was honking at me. I spied a phone booth and stood in the rain trying to find the number of the shop that had just fixed my car. The phone book was chained to the booth in a way that did not make it possible to actually open it. I found the number and called Fool's Auto Repair. It was now after five p.m. on a Friday, and I listened to a recorded message tell me that they would reopen Monday morning at seven. I called AAA and was towed home.

Following what I call The Repair Nightmare, I had CHECK OIL, tattooed on my left arm.

Following what I call The Repair Nightmare, I had CHECK OIL, tattooed on my left arm. I also compiled a list of helpful Auto Repair Tip-Offs to prevent others from making my mistakes. I have been told that no one would ever make mistakes like mine, but to be positive, I have put together a list. Auto repair tip-offs are those small subtle clues that scream "STOP. GO HOME. YOU ARE MAKING A BIG MISTAKE." Now that I am auto savvy, I will help others.

Auto Repair Tip-Offs

- Laughter. If at any point in your conversation with the repair crew they snicker, laugh or nudge each other, become suspicious.

- You get out of your car and there is no one there. The shop is open but empty. No one is available to check your car, speak with you or take your money. You start thinking "Just take my money and get it over with. Why also waste my time?"

- Old broken vehicles, referred to as 'junk cars' line the entrance to the shop. They have been there for decades. Parts? I may be wearing my I KNOW NOTHING t-shirt, but even I don't want these parts.

Two weeks after the Repair Nightmare, I had bumper stickers printed, HONK IF YOU HAVE RIPPED OFF PATRICIA FINN. This has attracted a large following. A network of mechanics, painters and salesmen has formed. Lasting friendships have been made. With personal growth in mind, what did

I learn from this experience? Stay home. If possible, stay inside. Do not drive to Miami. Do not drive. Do not get CHECK OIL tattooed on your arm.

TO THE PAST AND BEYOND

The Times They Are A Changin'—Bob Who?

I can remember when giving a bar of soap for a hostess gift was about as normal as giving a bowl of mud. Soap was soap, it was not an essential oil boutique item. We enjoyed a lovely white soap, famous for being the soap that floats, and a yellow floor soap which was kept in the basement. We also enjoyed an exciting new product that felt invigorating but was gone in a week. Thanks to the essential oil movement, soap has been elevated to the status of perfume. Don't get me wrong; I enjoy fragrances and I enjoy essential oils. I have an essential oil diffuser in my car, and one at home. However, there was once a time, not too long ago when we lived without them. Are they really essential? I know, 'essential' refers to the oil/plant relationship, but it brings home the point that along with everything else soap has changed. So, to set the record straight, and for all younger readers, handcrafted soap and eucalyptus oil were not always household items. We Ancients did enjoy fancy, packaged soap that was wrapped in pretty paper and gently placed into gift boxes by companies like Yardley and Coty. These were given as gifts at Christmas, usually from grandma or a loving auntie. The scents were exclusively lavender or rose.

Recently, I was eyeing a seven-dollar handcrafted bar of soap at a soap boutique and started to wonder if, well . . . if it killed germs. What about germs? Isn't that why I'm washing my hands, to kill the germs? (I have always been a troublemaker.) I decided to ask the soap crafter about the germ aspect, "I love the orange-almond, does it kill germs?" First a blank stare, then a quick analysis of who I might be in terms of convenient stereotypes. She is thinking something like, "Conservative. Rich. Clueless." She's partially right. I will never deny clueless and conservative. My response was classic me, "I'll take it, I love it, no worries, in fact, I'll take two." What's wrong with me? Germs? I just won't use it when I go to New York City and ride the subway. In fact, I think I'll look for a bar of the yellow floor soap for my trip to New York, unless it's been banned for killing more than germs.

What else has changed since my care-free childhood days? People are getting bigger. Vitamins must be working because the beds that my grandparents slept on were never any larger than Full. This loving but diminutive couple also slept on a horsehair mattress. You guessed right, horsehair was firm. Similar to sleeping on a slab of marble, there was no bouncing

What else has changed since my care-free childhood days? People are getting bigger.

on the bed at grandpa's house. Today's progression of mattress sizes has expanded to include Queen and King. Way back when, children slept on Twin and their parents slept on Full. Hmmm . . . connecting the dots, families were larger, too.

When I consider sharing a King size bed it would be something like, "Are you there? . . . I'm over here, where are you?" This scholarly and thorough analysis of beds reveals that grandpa was short and so was grandma because they both slept on one full-sized mattress. Just a little something to bring up in the next conversation where you want to quickly change the subject from politics to pointless. As for the transition from horsehair to memory foam-indisputable proof that today's products are better.

Born Blonde

I am old enough to remember when we had four hair color choices: blonde, brown, black and red. Grey is not a choice. I was born blonde and have adorable baby pictures to prove it. "So why the do-it-yourself hair color, Miss Pat?" Instead of turning grey, my hair turned brown. I don't know why and I don't care. Not to be a platform for any one product, I tried one that was easy, but I didn't like the results. I now use a different brand and I love it. I also love it when people comment on my hair. Did someone behind the frozen yogurt counter recently say, "I love your hair color; it looks so natural." Oh. Thanks. She may as well have said, "I love your hair color; it looks so dyed to perfection."

Shall we go down hair care memory lane? Let's start with home perms. Why did our mothers do this and do it to us their innocent, loving daughters? How well I remember going into the school bathroom to find my friend Cathy wearing a scarf and crying because her second-grade teacher wouldn't let her wear a scarf in the classroom. Underneath? Curls, curls, and more curls. Her mom had given her the home perm. It was a terrible season in female childhood. Every day there was another casualty and we could only stare and shake our heads knowing our turn would come too.

Shall we go down hair care memory lane?

Then we went from curls to straight. The word was out; So and So had ironed her hair! How dare she? What a rebel. The next day, we were all doing it. You set the iron on low, bend your head down to the ironing board and using a protective cloth you ironed it straight. So easy. That was also the year that one friend went blonde using Clorox. The results were questionable.

Far be it from me to brag but I was one of the first to curl my hair; nobody used rollers in the fifth grade but Miss Prissy Pat. And today? I cut my own hair. I part it in the back, pull it forward in two bunches and snip. When I told this to one of my son's friends her reply was, "That's very *Little House on the Prairie*." That's not necessarily the look I am after but if it is *Little House on the Prairie* it is *Little House on the Prairie*. I was hoping for something more sophisticated. Cottage in the Pines? Chateau by the Sea? But that's it, my bathroom sink and me, La Salon. I don't have the patience to sit and get my hair done and well, it is just too similar to being at the dentist. I am sitting and you are standing and it's the body language. "A drill, fill and a trim, please."

Two Cans And A String

I have never tried it, but I am told that two empty cans connected with a string will transmit sound. "Hello. Hello, are you there?" Two cans? No, my android. "I can't really hear you but thanks for calling. You sound like you are under water." My son is on his speaker phone walking the streets of New York City and "Hello?" I guess he's at the subway, there's no reception underground. The difficult part for senior minded me living in today's phone directed world is that I like singular concepts. One object for one activity. Phone—one object. Camera—one object. Calendar—one object. Clock—one object. Radio—one object. Game—one object that I take out, put away, and lose the pieces. Using the same device for a multitude of tasks is out of my comfort zone.

I invite you to reminisce and remember when a phone was only a phone. Growing up, it was common in our neighborhood for houses to have a small telephone room. Our next-door neighbor had a phone room under the main staircase. There was a built-in desk, a chair and of course the object in discussion—a phone. There was a door.

I invite you to reminisce and remember when a phone was only a phone.

You went inside, sat down and in quiet and privacy you made your calls. We didn't have that style in our house. Instead, in a day of one phone per family, we had a multitude of phones. There was a phone in the kitchen, one on the porch, phones in two home offices and in all bedrooms. For some reason there was a princess phone in the attic. No missing a call at our house.

"So, what's the point, Miss Pat?" Well, um, let me see, if I need to have a point it would be that a phone was a phone and only a phone. It was not a camera, a clock or a calendar. Because phones now share the arena with a cast of thousands, I can't hear my son when he calls. His phone is with him at all times. The reception stinks. Our calls get dropped. The phone part has been compromised because it is no longer just a phone.

May I now rant about responsibility and care? I must remember to plug my phone in at night. I must know where my phone is at all times. Is this a child? A pet? I know, it's my little buddy that goes with me wherever I go. Being somewhat of a rebel, I dare to go on walks without my phone. I have been known to drive to the store without my phone. This makes me feel brave, fearless, daring, and possibly stupid.

Lock-Lock

Ahaa the good ole' days. Remember when you didn't lock your door? I don't remember that. My parents always locked the house doors, and the key was conveniently left for me under the milk box. Milk box? One day, the key wasn't there so I climbed in the window. When I described to my parents how I scaled the bricks, pried the outer window open with a stick and knocked down the curtains as I jumped triumphantly to the kitchen floor, there was silence. I guess I wasn't supposed to do that.

My friends in New York City have seven locks on their apartment door. It takes thirty minutes to close up for the night. They had a visitor staying with them who woke up early, went for a walk and she not only didn't relock the prison gate, she left the door slightly ajar! You can imagine the confused host. The guest is gone, the door is open, hmmm . . . are you sure I didn't do that?

It is true, I struggle with locking doors. It comes from a fear of being locked out. Do I have my key? I not only have my key I have one in the car, one out of the car, one in a secret place, a back-up key hidden outside and one left with a friendly neighbor. I panic if I reach into my purse and can't immediately grasp my set of keys. I solved that problem and keep my purse keys in a separate zippered pouch. As for car keys, in addition to my key ring, there is a set hidden at home, a back-up in the glove compartment and one hidden in a place that no one knows about but me and my cats.

I am a hoarder of keys. With a can of WD-40 I manage to not be defeated by lock technology, but I panic when I have to open a door with a key. Fear of the unknown maybe? Will it open? Maybe "Yes" and maybe "No." Maybe I will be LOCKED OUT! This is my excuse for casually walking out of a door without closing or locking it. I have no idea how I became obsessive/compulsive about locks. Because I am lock-a-phobic, I was impressed when I saw a boy open his front door using his thumb. Wow. No key. No lock. I like that. Do I need a password?

Remember when you didn't lock your door?

Order in the Classroom

I searched my brain data base for a suitable subject to perform 'exploratory surgery' and I selected Catholic school. When I was in the first grade my parents lived in New York and they relocated from Queens to the north shore of Long Island, a move New Yorkers will recognize as a step up. While touring the local Catholic school, we happened upon a Christmas party in the cafeteria. When asked if I would like to go to St. Peter's Catholic school, my answer was an immediate Christmas party, "Yes."

In January, I developed a serious first grade attendance problem. The classroom was located in the basement of the school building. Basements in New York have poles conveniently placed throughout. Poles that I would desperately cling to while my mother attempted to pull me toward the classroom door. Hearing the commotion, a nun would come out and my struggle was over. The Sisters were an authority not to be challenged. Defeated, I was firmly led to my desk, still sniffling but submissive. And just what was this cruel fate? We wore uniforms, walked in a line, and sat in rows with our hands folded on top of the desk. We stood when spoken to or called on to answer. There was no noise. We ate in silence in the cafeteria. We played on a playground without equipment, or even balls. It was the church parking lot. Guess what—WE HAD FUN!

One day, for some reason unknown to me, during recess, I knocked on the door of the Rectory. I was about eight or nine years old, and the Rectory is where the priests live. The door was answered by a Chinese butler (this was not a poor parish) and I was quietly ushered inside. The Fathers were eating lunch and I was soon sitting at the table enjoying freshly baked popovers and answering an occasional question. The priests did not eat in silence but trust me it was a subdued atmosphere. Let me interject that none of this was within the range of normal. Children did not knock on the door of the Rectory. I have no idea what I was thinking but after additional years of being me, the best I can offer is that I wasn't thinking—I just did it. Behavior patterns start young.

In my neighborhood, my Catholic school friends and I were referred to as The Catholic Kids. I remember one non-Catholic parent being very upset thinking that this was somehow not appropriate. It never bothered us. After all, weren't we the Catholic kids? We went to Catholic school, we didn't eat meat on Friday, we went to confession on Saturday and fasted on Sunday morning until after communion. You don't get more Catholic than that. And then it happened! Mid-year in the fifth grade, my mother enrolled me in public school. Main Street School was the local elementary school and what the name lacked in creativity was accompanied by a culture that was foreign and confusing. Students ran from their desks when the bell rang. No one stood up when spoken to and where were the lines? Did I adjust? No. I will always be a product of Catholic school. I like quiet, order and structure. It was worth wearing a uniform, substituting sports with tap for boys and ballet for girls. We were not taught science, and there was no art or music or gym.

Today, I can read, write and occasionally do basic math. Who says the earth isn't flat? It looks flat to me, as I ballet step across the room to happily sort my earrings into neatly labeled zip lock bags.

I will always be a product of Catholic school. I like quiet, order and structure.

Don't Smile—Say "Cheese"

I am not excited about what technology has done for the world of photography. Last week I met a seventh grader who is learning Photoshop in school. That makes me feel inadequate. Photoshop, and phone/camera technology has enabled everyone to be a photographer, a videographer, and a pain in the shall I say—*neck*? Possibly, I have a bad attitude. Do the phone photographers ever consider that maybe I don't want to have my picture taken? Must I stop what I am doing so you can record it for being the moment that I was enjoying myself but had to stop to have my picture taken? Do I want to see the pictures on your phone? Your dog wearing sunglasses? Your cousin eating a sandwich? Her big toe? No, not really. Bad, Bad, Bad says the fussy old lady.

What about being able to see my grandchildren instantly on my phone with a video of them riding bikes, reading, playing and I even got to see my grandson's first steps. Priceless. I could easily change my tune and say that photo technology is wonderful especially if you are distant grandparenting.

Let's go back to when cameras were separate objects that were worn with a strap around your neck. When it was time to take a picture, you lifted it up, peered inside and focused using a nob. That was only step one. The next step was to rewind the film, remove it from the camera and bring it to the drug store. Yes, youngsters—the drug store. You left the film there and in about seven days the pictures were ready to be picked up. Aaah the good old days.

My favorite camera was the Polaroid, the camera that did it all. The Polaroid enabled you to take a picture and then after a short delay and some grunts the pictures magically emerged. I loved it. Instant gratification.

I like stuff, and technology has replaced stuff with electronic pictures of stuff. Obviously, the biggest example is online shopping. Remember the Mall? Stores are closing and this is getting scary. One of my best shopping memories was seeing an adorable four-year-old at a perfume counter testing every sample while wearing a hat she had picked up in the ladies' hat department. The tag was dangling in front. Pretty cute. Her mother was nowhere to be seen. You won't enjoy something like that shopping online. Yes, it is less tiring but what's all the energy for if not to roam the malls in search of happiness? Hmmm maybe I need to rethink this. Last weekend I was willing to stop what I was doing and go to a real store. I looked at real stuff, paid (gulp) real money. Best of all the shipping was free.

> *I like stuff, and technology has replaced stuff with electronic pictures of stuff.*

Wedding Bells

It is time to share something personal. I am going to reveal the truth about my first marriage. If thoughts like 'Who cares?' and 'What's the point?' come to mind, all I can do is encourage you to read on. I married Binky Murphy. We were outside, trespassing in a neighbor's vacant lot. I was seven. Binky was six. Hopefully by now he is using the name Vincent. CEO and Binky just don't go hand in hand. Binky was one of the seven Murphy kids who lived next door. We lived on Long Island in the suburbs. Binky's dad owned an advertising agency in Manhattan and like many of the dads he commuted into New York City on the Long Island railroad. I was friends with Binky's sister who was the ringleader of our little pack.

A wedding was serious fun. Binky's sister Cathy and I had trouble finding boys who would agree to play wedding. For the nuptial event, Cathy and I would dress up in Mrs. Murphy's full-length slips (I have no idea where she was while we raided her lingerie drawer). We made toilet paper flowers for our wedding bouquets. We knew that we needed a groom, so we took turns marrying Binky. The non-bride would officiate. My marriage to Binky was a planned event and Cathy chose the vacant lot. Cathy made a lot of the decisions. She grew up to be a mayor. I am still waiting for my grown-up identity to emerge. Queen? Secretly, I was disappointed that I was not marrying Cathy's older brother Kevin, but oh well.

Play was different in the 1950's. It was a safer world. The only rule set by our parents was to be home for dinner with little accountability for where we had been and what we had been doing. We lived in a very safe suburban neighborhood. The streets had almost no traffic, the houses were spacious; and the world was ours. We rode our bikes everywhere and had a lot of outdoor fun. Rarely did we play inside but when we did, Cathy's older brothers liked to play 'Chicken.' Cathy and I were the designated poultry. We were lifted on to their shoulders and told to try to push each other off. This may seem harmless except it was played in their upstairs hallway over an open stairwell. Her brothers also liked to put the smaller children, like Binky and me in their laundry dumbwaiter and send us from the third floor down to the basement.

Play was different in the 1950's. It was a safer world.

Mr. and Mrs. Murphy's bedroom had French doors that opened onto a roof patio. There was a protective ledge around the patio. Cathy and I thought it was hilarious to run onto the patio in our underwear, dance around and then laughing run back inside. None of this was too shocking since there were no people around and we were six years old but none the less, we thought it was very daring and funny.

Good things come to an end and our vacant lot weddings came to an abrupt halt the day a man appeared on the lot. I ran home, my heart pounding with fear. As for the dumbwaiter rides, those too came to a sudden stop the day Mr. and Mrs. Murphy walked in while the adventure was in progress. The dumbwaiter was a broken wooden box on a pulley with a fraying rope. Did I say it was a safer world?

HI-HO HI-HO

Dear Reader

Senior jobs, I just don't know. When I weigh the pros and cons, the jury is still out. Today, I am sick and confined to the house for three more days, just bed and books. Being over sixty and teaching in a Head Start program is a challenge. It is too hot to venture outside, especially with a low-grade fever. I am teaching in Arizona and it is 114 degrees in the shade, if you can find shade. My doctor has told me to stay inside, rest, and lose my mind. I never thought of myself as a particularly social person. My self-image has always been a female Maverick type, independent, a loner, not a girl who moves with the pack. I am my own best friend. No wonder I am losing it.

When I consider the daily interactions that I have at work, I am surprised that the absence of human contact has been so painful. My day-to-day conversations with the other teachers are not deep or meaningful. "I'll break at noon, when do you want to go to lunch?" "I'll do Circle Time. Do you have any glue?" Proof that the lonely human spirit can be filled with the simplest day-to-day dribble.

Let me go comfortably back in literary time to better acquaint you with the stresses of my daily life, none of which cause in any serious harm. 19th Century British novels had a tradition of 'talking' to the

Proof that the lonely human spirit can be filled with the simplest day-to-day dribble.

reader. Authors would discuss the plot in a conversational tone. "And now Dear Reader, I know you are in suspense to discover what happens to Patience, but we first need to visit her sister who is vacationing in a small seaside cottage." Dear Reader, is transported to the seaside and discovers that Elizabeth has become addicted to opium on a recent trip to China after the loss of her only true love, Sir Michael who was blown apart in the Crimean War.

With this style in mind, I will describe one aspect of my workday—Potty Training. It is an essential activity, cruelly overlooked by academia, the press, and other teachers. This task should be given more prestige. Who of you reading this would like to be wearing a pull-up? Point made.

All children are beautiful, but at twenty-four months they all fit into the category called Terrible Two. Terrible Two is not rare or selective or an unusual occurrence. It is universal. And so Dear Reader, please enjoy Chapter One of *Arizona Days*.

The Universal "No"

"Potty time," I cheerfully sing out. "No," snaps two-year-old Little Dove with a look of total hatred.

She quickly dashes under the table where I will have to perform the begging on my hands and knees ritual. "Potty is fun. Come out. Miss Pat wants you to go potty then I will take you to the playground. All of your friends are there, but you need to go potty first." Little Dove takes off both of her shoes and throws them at me. Plan #2 is now put into effect. According to the teacher manual, all negative behavior is to be ignored. I sit down and begin rolling playdough meat balls and line them up in a neat row. I attempt to engage her interest by singing Humpty Dumpty with a rap beat. She is not impressed. Playdough is not exciting enough to coax her to come out from under the table, so I chose to alternately juggle and blow bubbles.

After five years of teaching preschool, I can do this. It works. A sweet little girl is now standing at my side trying to pull the bubble wand out of my hand. "Go potty, then I will give you the bubbles, you have to go potty first." The Bible verse 'Train up a child . . . ' comes to my mind as she walks obediently into the bathroom. Could this ability to flip flop behavior be the start of multiple personality syndrome? I consider the fame associated with writing a book about this theory as Little Dove and I now walk happily, hand in hand toward the playground. At nap time, I refresh myself by creating titles for the above-mentioned book. My get me out of here with literary success, break through treatise on the universality of negativity. Possible title: *The Universality of*

Negativity, too formal, I want this to be an easy read for the non-professional. I consider the title, *Two Forever.* No. That sounds too romantic, I will think of another title. This book will be a best seller and hailed as a hallmark in psychiatric literature. I will travel on national speaking tours and leave pull-ups forever behind. *Forever Behind?* No behind. No pull-ups. I will have a new focus—the human brain. What about, *Crazy—No?* Too casual but moving in the right direction. *Stuck at Two & Who Are You?* Too Dr. Seuss.

I will put the title on hold and write the book first. A painful decision, picking a title is inspiring. Instead, I will write a little tune to prepare to write my break-through dissertation on the human mind. And so Dear Reader:

This is my song.
I'm in the bathroom, all the day long.
When you teach 'Twos' it is plain and it's clear,
It's not just your paycheck that is in arrears.

When my fever broke, I was told by the school nurse that I had contracted hoof and mouth disease. Hoof and mouth was traveling through the Baby Room at our school, and sadly it is the elderly (not me of course) and infants that are in the category of most susceptible to infection. In vain I protested, "But . . . I'm not a horse." I returned to the classroom unsure if I had a foot or a hoof, but very sure that it was time to book a fast flight back to Florida and leave Arizona behind.

Fifty Hour a Week Toys

If you could bring a toy to work, what would it be? Think. 'Dress Down' day has gotten boring and old. It's time to liven up the workplace. I recommend adding Toy Day to the calendar. It will reduce work-related stress. You might even consider a professional 'Show and Tell' event. Would you bring a stuffed animal? A truck? A train? Oh, so you have stopped playing with toys have you, well it's time to start again. Anyone who works fifty hours a week deserves a toy.

What toy would I bring? Probably my all-time favorite, a soft, pink rubber ball that fits perfectly in the palm of my hand. I can throw it and catch it and it bounces well. Here are some toy choices for professionals I have worked with and what I would expect them to bring to Toy Day. A slinky for the salesman. A truck for the landscaper. The CEO's might bring yo-yos but will need instruction and practice. The massage therapist would bring a frisbee.

To build my defense for returning to the world of toys, I ask you to think back to the days when Lincoln logs, Legos, and mini kitchen sets were a part of your happy lives. My Toy Day theory is based on the premise that toys are relaxing and even more relaxing than watching TV. Like many adults I have spent evenings unwinding in front of my television set, sometimes too stressed to even change the channel. Thumb exhaustion. If watching TV works to relieve work-day stress, why are there so many sleep aids being advertised? I plop on the couch and then toss under the covers. I thought I was tired but why am I not sleeping? Weren't the true crime shows relaxing?

My formula for destressing is to bring out the toys. You don't remember how to play with toys? You think toys are for children only? Nope. Not anymore. Go into your bedroom, close the door, sit on the floor and dump out the Legos. Feeling more aggression than snap together construction can solve? No problem. Hammer pegs. Anything to unwind without succumbing to the lure of the couch.

I know about workday stress. It can be very 'challenging' as we say in today's world of political correctness. I recently had a high stress job, and it was difficult to leave the cares of the day behind. One day, I stopped at a stop sign and sat waiting for the light to change. The next morning, I opened a bag of kitty litter and poured it into the cat food bowls. I looked at it and thought, "This doesn't look right."

Why the disfunction? My mind was solving problems that should have

I know about workday stress. It can be very 'challenging' as we say in today's world of political correctness.

ended at five o'clock. What a day! My laptop warped and there was a bump in the middle of the keyboard. I dropped something on my foot and my big toenail might not grow back. In the morning when I unlocked my office, someone had entered and left a broken chair on top of my chair. There was a note attached. It said, "Fix this." I was the interim school principal. Has anyone seen my pink rubber ball?

Dare to Decorate

Seasonal decorating is fun. I enjoy being creative, so I am mixing purple paint with white glue to paint paper mâché eggs. The plan is to avoid the messy Easter egg dyes. Using a wire spoon you lower eggs into hot water where a colored pill has neatly dissolved in the bowl of your choice. All within bowls, rarely splashing, never dripping. What was I thinking? Why did I think a glue / paint concoction would be less messy? Purple, purple everywhere. And the glorious result? Eggs that are shamefully streaked and splotchy—a kindergarten mess.

Why am I coloring eggs without the excuse of a child? I am determined to have something seasonal on my desk at work. I call it DIY pride and I am always ready to show off my artsy craftsy skill set. Admittedly, my fall gold painted pumpkin was a hard act to follow; but the vase filled with pinecones and glitter was a good December statement.

I am determined to have something seasonal on my desk at work.

Holiday decorating can be very competitive and 'the more the better' is often the approach. Christmas can become the clash of the humble wreath versus the life size reindeer. It's a hard choice. I like both ends of the decorating spectrum. This is an opportunity to be creative and have fun. Being both lazy and on a budget, I marvel at the work that goes into some holiday decorating. It took me half a day to add bells and a few fake poinsettia to a plastic wreath.

Next on the holiday décor calendar is the egg season. I rule out bunnies and go with colored eggs. I am a realist and reject decorating with rabbits that are carrying colored eggs. Show me a bunny that lays eggs, and I will give you a chicken that hops. My plan is to put my miserable blotched eggs into a wicker basket, add a few silk flowers and fortunately it is only a few weeks before I can trash it and start a summer tribute to my crafty self-indulgence.

Summer. Summer. Summer. How will I decorate for summer? A beach ball? A shovel and pail? I'm in Florida, so how about a lovely bowl of sweat? Summer in Florida is a paradigm that awakens memories of having my air conditioning go out. It was the weekend. The maintenance man brought me a dehumidifier and said, "I feel your pain." I expected a fan. A dehumidifier? I guess he couldn't feel my pain without bringing me a token gift of some sort. Not a solution, no solutions were to be had until Monday, but looky look—I can plug it in—fans get plugged in! I can adjust a dial, just like a fan! Now I will be able to say, "Maintenance came right away, they brought me what they had." How about a plunger, do you have a plunger? Light bulb? I'll take anything. Don't worry if it has nothing to do with my not having any air.

I survived that hot summer weekend. I lived through it, sustained by thoughts of dehydrated pioneer women before me. I have always had the attitude that it is better to be too hot than too cold. Did people really live here before air conditioning? In Florida we measure time three ways: B.C., A.D., and Pre A.C.

The DMV and Me

'Retirement' and 'job', isn't that an oxymoron? I spent half of my adult life at home and then became a 'displaced homemaker.' I like to call it 'misplaced.' I had my first desk job at the age of sixty-five. Was I retired? Do I qualify as a retired working professional since I got such a late start? Sitting for eight hours was a new experience and I was quick to learn that lunchtime was a good time to do small errands. I needed to replace my driver's license, but was that a small errand? How do I describe my visit to the DMV? It reminds me of something my late aunt once told me. She said that when she watered the lawn with a rotating sprinkler, the neighbors would sell tickets. I could have made a fortune at the DMV. I raced downtown, thinking—new license? Easy breezy. Employment had given me a new 'can do' attitude.

At first, everything went remarkably well, a convenient parking spot, a short line, I answered a few questions. They didn't ask for proof of ID or address, the questions that I was prepared to answer with documents, passport, mail, everything to prove my ability to be a responsible citizen and driver. I was prepared, prepared, prepared.

All was going well until I was asked, "Do you wear glasses for driving?" I became immediately nervous. I felt myself becoming transparent. Stammering "Don't you want to see my photo ID? Here, look, I have a tax document with my address." Again, but with more emphasis, "Do you wear glasses for driving?" "Well, yes but, well no, the lens keeps falling out." The clerks whisper and give each other 'a look.'

I was beckoned over to the eye test machine. The chart had three columns and seven lines. "Read line five." I proudly read across the first two columns. Oddly, the third column had no letters, it was just white paper. Strange. "Come over here please." I now had the complete attention of everyone in the room. That was not too amazing because it is a small town. Five people were in rapt attention to this drama. I went to the second machine. It was the same scenario, I read across two columns and the third column had no letters. I glanced at a clock and saw that I had exactly twenty-five minutes left to finish this project, drive back to the office and be sitting at my desk calm, relaxed and smiling. Maybe doing this during my lunch break was not such a good idea.

I was told, "Go to your car and get your glasses." Reduced to child-like obedience I went to my car, got my glasses, and popped in the left lens. I wanted my license now and I didn't want another eye appointment, new glasses, the whole package that seemed to be looming in my immediate future. With the entire room in rapt attention, I covered my right eye as directed, then I dropped my purse. "Wait a minute, there is a reason for this. It's my mono-vision problem!" I quickly covered my left eye; the lens fell onto the floor and instantly the letters appeared in the blank column. With triumph in my voice, I read N S X T H! Applause broke out behind me. Smiles from the folks behind the counter. Yes! I did it! I can get my license! I had ten minutes to get back to work, and no time to explain mono-vision.

Coffee—Office Style

Coffee. Coffee. Coffee. The Coffee Pot, the Coffee Maker, the Coffee Machine. Life is good as long as the precious liquid is supplied on time and without flaw. Computers, copiers, fax machines, none can match the importance of this revered Office Shrine. My foremost responsibility at a retirement office job was to see that the coffee pot was full. For reasons I will not disclose, I was Office Administrator and not CEO. Office Administrator is fancy for receptionist. Receptionist is derived from the word receive, and I received about three people a week.

I soon learned that office work was not a good choice for me.

I soon learned that office work was not a good choice for me. I was expected to handle problems that were outside my comfort zone. My comfort zone was the area immediately surrounding my desk. My desk was next to a large window with a beautiful view. I stared out the window a lot. I organized my desk a lot. I rearranged the office entry room furniture. I organized the staff kitchen. With approval, I finally brought in knitting. Apparently, my predecessor sat and made jewelry. During my first week at the job, there was a mini celebration for one of the business owners. Cake and coffee were served in the conference room. I took my cake to the conference table and sat down. Big mistake. Everyone else was standing cocktail party style. In office culture you don't sit. I was from the world of classroom teaching. Teachers sit whenever possible.

I was very good at being friendly, but the cheery disposition was not enough the day I had to write the word BROKEN and tape it on to The Coffee Shrine. Unable to resist giving it that personal touch, and not wanting my preschool teacher training to go to waste; I drew a sad face with tears dripping into an empty cup. I did have the business savvy to schedule a visit from the coffee service for the next day, but sorry folks, if you want coffee in the morning you will need to bring it with you.

The next day, when I arrived at 8:00 a.m. the sign was down, and the coffee pot was half full. "Oh. It's working." What could be the meaning of this surprising change of events? Why did one early bird individual ignore my sign and be so bold as to press the START button? Does that person have anything to do with the coffee pot not working the day before? All necessary plugs were plugged into all necessary sockets, of course I checked that. I could ask the risk-taking individual who dared to defy my BROKEN sign and push the START button, why they considered that there was a small chance it would work, when I, the keeper of the coffee pot had declared that The Coffee Maker was broken. Why would they push that START button?

We will close this with what can only be called a 'cliff hanger.' Does the coffee pot continue to work through-out the day or does it blank out midafternoon? Does Office Administrator Air Head discover why the machine stopped and then returned to functioning order without or perhaps with human intervention? Did supernatural forces attack human machinery? You will never know.

In Keeping With Love and Marriage

Summer and weddings go hand in hand. When I think about summer weddings, I am reminded of the lovely Bed & Breakfast Inn where I sought refuge following a serious car accident. Decorated with costly antiques, and landscaped with hedges of blooming jasmine, it was a popular wedding venue. I arrived at the Inn wounded, but I left happy and healed. Why? The answer is easy. After several weeks of enjoying myself as a guest, I transitioned from guest to Innkeeper.

Occasionally there were two wedding events happening at the same time. One reception would be in the lavish reception hall and the other in the Victorian house with a dramatic staircase for the bride's entrance. It was not unusual to have a horse drawn carriage waiting at the end of a long arch of jasmine to whisk the married couple away to…this part was not clear. The carriage probably took them around the block where they were transferred to a car, but it was impressive.

Soon after my transition to Innkeeper my motto became 'expect the unexpected.' Unexpected? Late one Saturday night, instead of going to her room, a guest stumbled into the library and for some reason couldn't find her way out. Did I mention that she was naked? Bare to the bone. Thoughtfully she had wrapped herself in a tablecloth. Could I help her find her way? But of course.

Sunday brunch was a big event. Set in the dining room with a lovely fireplace, it was often the departure meal for a weekend wedding. One Sunday, five minutes before the breakfast guests were due to arrive, I heard a commotion; a weird noise. I rushed into the dining room and a bird's nest with newly hatched and squealing birds had fallen down the chimney. I called the chef. I might be the Innkeeper, but I am still Miss Prissy Pat. He carried the nest to safety.

I enjoyed being the Innkeeper, and I learned new recipes and honed my kitchen skills. I learned to make crepes, cheese grits and a French toast casserole that if I sold it on the street, I would be a millionaire. Occasionally, we opened the front porch for an outdoor breakfast experience. One morning a woman was very concerned that there might be ants if she ate on the porch. I assured her that I had never seen any ants and that we served breakfast there frequently. There was no need to worry. At the buffet table she reminded me that she was worried about ants. Again, I assured her that there were no ants on the porch. Less than five minutes after leaving with a plate piled high with food, she came back, held up her plate and pointed to an ant. How could that happen? How did she know? Did ants follow her through life? How did one ant find its way to her table and onto her plate?

Another morning after a late-night reception, I was scrambling eggs, when a young man came into the kitchen and stood sleepily at my side. "Yes, yes. How can I help you?" Whispering, he beckoned me outside and then slowly, ever so slowly told me that the cottage where he and the bride were staying was on fire. What! Wake up buddy! I ran to the cottage, it was not ablaze, but it was filled with smoke. The bride was carried out to the yard, windows were opened, and it all had a happy ending. Back in the kitchen, my eggs were still on the stove. When I told the guests that it was a three-hour egg and would be ready soon, everyone smiled.

> *I ran to the cottage, it was not ablaze, but it was filled with smoke.*

Occasionally alarms went off at critical dramatic moments, but usually everything flowed. Well, sort of flowed. Twenty minutes before one big wedding, "What's that terrible smell?" A dead opossum was under the house and stinking like a skunk. No problem, not for *this* Innkeeper. Dead opossum? Bring it on. I was no longer a weary and injured traveler, my bones were healed, my spirits were lifted. I had become Innkeeper Invincible.

Raccoon Rukus

We all have had scary moments, but this one is unique. I was held hostage by a pack of raccoons. Working alone in the office of an upscale Bed and Breakfast Inn, I left the front door open and went upstairs. When I came back, five raccoons were running from room to room. I was prepared for rude guests but not raccoons. I screamed and jumped on top of a desk. At first, I wasn't sure what to do. Should I call 911? I didn't want them arrested. I decided to call the owner for moral support. "I know you can't help me, but the office is full of raccoons." I screamed again, and they ran out. I locked the door. Thinking I was safe, I prepared to leave, but the saga wasn't over. Five raccoons were sitting outside the door looking at me through the glass. I was trapped!

There is a history to this encounter. The lead raccoon and I go back. Last spring after closing the B & B's main house, I saw him lurking on the roof in the shadows waiting for me to leave. Clever, but not cleverer enough. "I see you, Mr. Raccoon, and I know you are watching and waiting for me to leave." The dark relationship had begun. In

> *"I know you can't help me, but the office is full of raccoons."*

early summer, in broad daylight a mother raccoon paraded in front of me with her offspring. Now a family, the raccoons had abandoned garbage can scavenging. They were feasting nightly from the over-flowing bowls of cat food our staff provided for the parking lot cats.

The night the raccoons came inside, they were looking for cat food, became confused and started running wildly to get back out. I do not accept the cliché, "They were more frightened than you." First, how does anyone know how frightened they were, and secondly, I will tell you how frightened I was. There were five of them and one of me and I am not aggressive. Although I am living in the South, I do not want to eat coon. Someone once told me, "They were eating coon back then in North Florida." Well, I may be in North Florida but if I can't buy it at the grocery store, I don't want it for dinner. Coon has never been a choice. The coons were clearly not the ones in danger that night. Were they cute? Well, it is sort of like snow. I like to look at snow from inside a warm house. I will watch Mr. Raccoon through a window, as he deftly dumps garbage over the yard, but I do not want to see him inside. Humans in—Coons out.

I slept in the office that night and cautiously made my way home at the break of dawn. Being a thinking woman, I thoughtfully considered the problem. The B & B cleaning crew had been filling the cat bowls to overflowing. They were feeding the kitties and the neighborhood coons. I gave the crew a measuring cup and I encouraged them to use restraint. I also had a sign made which now hangs by the office door:

> In the Morning, Night, and Noon
> Feed the Cats and Not the Coon

Wondering if I had somehow brought the attack on with what some folks would call 'bad karma' I stayed awake for weeks, tossing and turning. I don't think so. I like animals. I have cats. Last year, I petted my neighbor's dog. I even enjoy waking up to the sound of a rooster that mysteriously found its way to the park adjacent to my apartment. No, I can't think of anything that I may have done to initiate a random, violent attack on innocent, peace loving me. I will use this encounter to write my first novel: *The Revenge of The Raccoons.*

OPINIONATED OPINIONS

Weather or Not Here I Come

Welcome to my weather channel. Whether you have experienced Florida rain or not, that is where we will start. The rain in Florida is like snow up North. You prepare for the rain, understand the rain and realize that it is a whole lot more than water. It is torrential. If it rains while you are driving, the experience is like having someone sit on the hood of your car and direct a hose full force at your windshield. If you are crazy enough to be out walking in the rain, umbrellas are essential but not always affective. I recommend a large golf size umbrella with a wooden handle and wind vents. The small collapsible purse size umbrellas are unthinkable when it comes to Florida rain. In Florida it can be raining on one side of the street and not on the other. Coming from Long Island where the rain falls evenly and lasts all day, Florida rain was an adjustment.

The topic of rain naturally leads to hurricanes and I experienced several hurricanes while living on a Florida Key. The worse one was a storm that was called the 'No Name Storm' because it never made it to full hurricane status. This nameless monster washed away a beach cottage, flooded my street and caused me to leave in the middle of the night. On my way to safety, I stopped at my parent's house where an aunt and an uncle were staying. My uncle was very old school and would not come out to see what I wanted until he had shaved, showered and put on a clean and presentable outfit. No running outside in a bathrobe and slippers for this uncle. I sat and waited while the water rose; and the winds blew, and well . . . manners are manners.

I will now skyrocket to Arizona where the weather is so hot, it is not life sustaining. It is a possible prelude for hell, with the potential of being an affective evangelical tool. I plan to make that suggestion should the opportunity come up. People like to ask if the Arizona heat was comfortable because there is no humidity. At 118 degrees who cares? Walking outside was like walking in an oven.

People like to ask if the Arizona heat was comfortable because there is no humidity. At 118 degrees, who cares?

Moving forward, I will rant about the wind. I don't like wind and I especially don't like it in my face. I avoid motorcycles, fast rides and stay inside on windy days. In high school, I told this to a guy friend, and he looked at me with disgust and called me a baby. It was not a 'Hey baby.' Growing up (and I *did* grow up) we spent our summers in Maine and like clockwork every first week in September we experienced a hurricane. Very windy.

In New York, I loved walking in the falling snow, especially at night. Snow is a wonderful, amazing gift. I left before I ever had to drive on this amazing, wonderful gift. Somewhere in the distance, I hear, "Say goodnight, Gracie," so I will close by saying that life would be dull if the weather were always the same. I like to be surprised. I don't watch the weather channel or check my phone to see the radar. It is sort of like pregnancy before sonograms.

Thank You for the Lovely Plant

Oh, for the love of house plants! They bring the beauty of the outdoors inside, inside to slowly die. When someone hands me a house plant, I softly whisper into its abundant foliage, "I'm sorry, I am *really* sorry." So many blooming baskets doomed. Today lovely but soon to be shriveled, lifeless, dried stick, another casualty for my backyard house plant graveyard. On the other hand, are plants really supposed to be inside? Climate control, stale air, strange lighting, no bugs. At least I hope no bugs. Plants belong outside.

Please do not fall into the trap of thinking that they enhance your indoor environment. No, no, no. First, they have to be watered. Second, they have to be watered. My indoor plants are in hanging baskets because I have cats. Cats like to eat the leaves and dig in the dirt. Inspired by the Hanging Gardens of Babylon, my solution to the cat /plant problem is to put indoor plants in hanging baskets. They are given a healthy start which lasts about a month before they plunge into a rapid encounter with death. "Oh. I need to water the plants. Soon. I *will* water . . ." Then . . . I stop looking, I have forgotten. I can't watch.

> *Plants belong outside.*

The plant watering problem is more complex than it might appear. Watering my house plants involves standing on a small step ladder because the plants are in hanging baskets. The step ladder is kept in the garage on a hook. Once I have brought the step ladder inside, I must fill the watering can and one time is never enough, but that's okay because I am climbing down from the step ladder and dragging it from plant to plant. With each step down, I go to the sink and refill the watering can. Down the ladder, walk to the sink. Up the ladder. Down the ladder, walk to the sink. Up the ladder.

One day the scores of shriveled greenery got their revenge. What I am about to write is graphic in nature and reader discretion is advised. There is a plant that will not fit in a hanging basket. A bayonet plant is nature's weapon of destruction. The name should give you a clue to its shape and size. This dangerous human predator has no blooms, and no leaves. It's rare lack of beauty lies in the abundance of two to four-foot-high stalks that end in a dagger shaped spike. Why would anyone have a plant like this? Why would anyone keep a plant like this inside by their front door? Now that I think about it, *who gave me this plant*?

In Arizona, I had an indoor planter filled with bayonet plants, a weak tribute to the cactus foliage I never liked. One day, I reached down and grabbed a bag that I was taking out with me and Wamo! A bayonet pierced my eye. I leaned right into it. I will not discuss the pain, the intense, heart stopping pain, as I staggered then collapsed. Why did this happen? It happened because once upon a time, a long time ago, someone, somewhere, decided that it was a good idea to bring plants inside. That decision led to my being stabbed in the eye by a bayonet plant. If you come to visit do not be surprised, my house is the one with the large sign at the door:

WELCOME—NO GUNS—NO PLANTS

Please Pass the Dressing

Occasionally, Harry Houdini stripped naked to prove that there was nothing up his sleeve. We like to say that clothes make the man. We dress for success, or in Harry's case, we undress. Our language shows the importance we put on clothing. The salad is dressed. The bones are bare, we speak of the bare facts, the naked truth. Clothes, clothes and no clothes. Why do I have such an interest in clothes? I recently discovered the Baby Book that my parents kept for me. It recorded important moments; when I took my first step, my first smile, and not too surprising it recorded my first word. It was 'dress.' I called it a 'fess.' According to the Baby Book, I insisted on wearing a fess after nap. Overalls in the morning, fess in the afternoon. I haven't changed much.

How we cover up and what we wear or don't wear says a lot about who we are. A friend from Hawaii told me that she grew up surfing naked. This was not too surprising after seeing a photo of her and her cousin bending over in their T-Back swimsuits. My father was so modest that he dressed in his small walk-in closet. He never wore shorts, and he always wore a fedora hat.

Hats are important. Court Jesters wore unique and colorful outfits, but it was their hats that added the final touch that said—Ridiculous. I for one, would like to see this style in Washington. The Capitol Jester? What about the Dunce Cap? After a few years of teaching, this one has my full support.

Uniforms can be wonderful unifiers. Police, firemen, and military uniforms—good. School uniforms—not good. Bell Hops were before my time but thanks to old movies, I get to see short men wearing classic Bell Hop uniforms. A cross between a marching band and the Foreign Legion, who designed those?

Clothes and culture are close cousins.

Clothes and culture are close cousins. I am old enough to remember when wearing white on the tennis court was the only permissible color. Clorox anyone? I live in a retirement town and when I go to the supermarket my fellow shoppers at least *look* to be well off. Looking well off in a Florida resort town means that you are wearing designer exercise clothes. The dress is casual, but upscale casual. Always out of style, I am wearing my after-nap fess.

Big Bad Kids

Today, I met my friend Kate at an outdoor café for a coffee chit-chat. She wanted me to meet her because she had to unload. This is what she said, "I have an interesting relationship with my adult children. I do everything they tell me to, and frankly I'm a pretty good kid. Daily, I walk the fine line between humiliate and humble. Humble—good. Humiliate—not good."

Yesterday, Kate's daughter was scolding, scolding, scolding. "She had me on the phone for over thirty minutes and would not stop long enough for me to offer any type of defense. By the time she finished, I'd forgotten what I wanted to say. She was relentless. When will I ever get it right? *It* can be anything from sending an email to managing my finances. I don't think I am going to change; why can't she focus on my good points?"

This is not an uncommon problem. It seems to be everywhere. I overheard a woman from a different ethnic background, say she was going to move out of her daughter's house and into a tent on family land to escape the nagging. She had been invited to live with her daughter but after three months, her bags were packed, and she was ready to go.

How does this role reversal happen? It happens mostly to moms and especially to moms who no longer have a dad to filter the noise. Now that they are grown, our grown children want to be our parents. Well-meaning adults are parenting the parent.

> *Now that they are grown, our grown children want to be our parents.*

Kate ended her daughter's phone call, "Well thanks for your input, I have to go, I'm about to crash into a tree." I am a pessimist when it comes to solving family drama, but I did manage to give my friend some advice. First, I tried to soothe her hurt feelings by telling her she was a peacemaker. "Yes," she sniffled, "But what makes it so tricky, is that the criticism is usually right. It's valid, but maybe I shouldn't have to hear it." Always willing to comfort a friend, I offered, "Don't worry, maybe you'll go deaf."

So, to the 'Kates' of this world, I commiserate. I offer compassionate condolences, words of encouragement and a simple word of advice. When they scold, scold, scold—listen, listen, listen, but with the phone away from your ear. Obviously, not something I have ever done. I also like the tent idea.

Ahh Micanopy!

I need to get away. It is time to come up with a travel plan that will accommodate both my limited budget and my fuss budget taste. What should I do? Think Miss Pat, *think*. I know, I will go to Micanopy! Historic Micanopy in North Central Florida, seat of my two-year long retirement. Quaint towns are frequently compared with Mayberry from the 1960's *Andy Griffith Show*. Micanopy is Mayberry.

You've never heard of Micanopy? Let me introduce you. Listed as one of America's top ten small quaint towns by the Huffington Post, Historic Micanopy is one charming block of small shops and a few eateries. In 1991, the movie *Doc Hollywood* was filmed there. The businesses are mostly antique shops with treasures that range from beautiful furniture to "What is this dusty thing?" Micanopy has a gazebo, a museum, a one room library, and a mansion that may be haunted.

Micanopy remains unspoiled because of the plumbing. All of this loveliness is on well and septic. Restaurants and bars can't accommodate the necessary toilet flushing and dish washing. Sad, I guess

Micanopy remains unspoiled because of the plumbing.

things will just have to remain small and cozy. Please don't think that visitors go hungry; there is food in Micanopy but on a small scale with limited seating. There are three places to eat and enjoy whatever your slow southern heart desires, four if you include Pearl's at the gas station.

Pearl's has a counter and inside tables. To enter Pearl's you must walk past men who sit on benches outside the front door. They are retired. It is easy to wonder if they ever worked but they came early, will leave late and sitting in front of Pearl's is a way of life.

What's on the menu at Pearl's? Pulled pork of course, this is the South, fried chicken, and very yummy cheese grits. Come for dinner; but eat fast because the kitchen closes at seven. If gas station dining is not your cup of tea, Micanopy offers more than dining at Pearl's.

On the ground floor of Shady Oak there is an ice cream parlor which serves sandwiches and home baked treats. What is Shady Oak? After living at Shady Oak for two years, I am still unsure. Frank is the owner and he built Shady Oak in 1990. He was the lead carpenter and is now proprietor extraordinaire. Shady Oak is a three-story plantation style building with a wraparound porch. It was once a B & B. Shady Oak has a beautiful gift shop, a stained-glass art studio and an ice cream parlor. Shady Oak is where local musicians play bluegrass music on the porch while the residents and tourists sit and relax.

Warning: Don't let Frank see you sitting on the porch swings marked FOR SALE.

There is an eatery next to Shady Oak that is eclectic with a capital E. Is this a cafe or a flea market? Five or six outside tables are tucked among a collection of . . . interesting stuff. There are one or two tables inside and it is worth going inside to discover treasures that range from an old radio to pretty pieces of antique china.

My favorite place for coffee and a snack is the Mosswood Farm Store and Bakehouse, which I refer to as The Bakery. A rustic cottage serving delicious coffee and baked goods, you can eat inside—there are two small tables or out back. I recommend the almond bear claw.

Micanopy is a popular destination for bike clubs, car clubs, retirees, and non-thrill seekers. On the weekend, tourists happily stroll carrying ice cream cones but not packages. Rarely have I seen people leaving the shops laden down with boxes and bags. How do the small shops survive? Oh my gosh—they need my help!

The Cost of Living, or Not

Recently, I was blown away by the cost of a new luxury car. Not that I am shopping for one, but it took me by surprise. *From* $125,950? I have worked in sales, so I know what the word 'from' is about. Now the options kick in. Do you want a sunroof? Do you want four tires? Do you want the doors to open? The good news is that this car comes with a lifetime repair guarantee. Generous, but what about collision? I always need to prepare for that. How did a tree get here overnight? Or the neighbor's car, rudely parked within a hundred feet of mine? Scratches, dings, bumps, I think I had better stick with my Chevy.

I am at an age when the price of everything seems colossal. From walnuts to cars, why are things not the same price that they were forty years ago? Have my resources increased to keep up? Someone told me the other day that they expect to pay $100 to take a family of four out to lunch. That's more than my weekly grocery budget. A magazine is $10.00? Where am I? Folks, I am in The Senior Zone. Some people in The Senior Zone will not tip more than $5.00 regardless

> *I am at an age when the price of everything seems colossal.*

of the bill. It is a part of what I call Separation Preparation. "Well, it's a good thing I am passing soon because it is just too expensive to be here."

Unfortunately, it is also too expensive to die. I'm a planner, so I checked the cost of a traditional burial. I will have to wait until the price comes down. Several years ago, I lost a few readers when I discussed my surprise discovery that coffins have become a new creative art form. Thanks to too much free time and the internet, I learned that people have gone all out with creative coffin designs making it a final artistic statement. Entrepreneurial companies have designed coffins to fit every taste and final wish, bragging that they are, "Bringing quirky color to a sad time." There are coffins painted to look like the Tardis, a box of chocolate, leopard skin, a football, flowers. Why not? I like to be creative, why not take advantage of an assembled group of friends and family to make a final statement? The Bible refers to the death of Believers as being 'asleep.' Taking 'asleep' as my cue, I would have a custom coffin painted to look like a bed with a pillow and a fluffy comforter. A perfect match for the epitaph, "Here Lies a Dreamer."

Uh-Oh Here Come the Dolls

Do you ever think about dolls? Do you consider that they are little imitation people that children manipulate? May I ruffle the feathers of your memory, rob you of your favorite dolly and invite you to reject the very foundation of the child / doll relationship? No, I won't do that because I still have my favorite dolls. Are you surprised? Blame my mother; she saved them.

My favorite doll was not an American doll. An aunt who liked to spoil me, visited Japan and brought me back a doll that instead of changing the doll's clothes you changed her elaborate wig. It was a Japanese theater doll, and now I know that 'she' was probably a 'he' but that doesn't change my love for this doll and the fact that sixty years later it is kept in my top dresser drawer.

Dolls can be creepy, especially when they are voodoo dolls that are on poles outside of a daughter's apartment.

Dolls can be creepy, especially when they are voodoo dolls that are on poles outside of my daughter's apartment. Yes, that really happened. It's a crazy world and the voodoo dolls were unexpected. What

21st century suburban mom expects voodoo dolls? Once again, I may be out of touch. I remember the day when I was approached by a stranger who decided that I was a good candidate for a curse. She took my hands and proceeded to 'incant' all over me. She must have been a novice because that was years ago and although life hasn't been perfect, I have not experienced anything that could be called a curse. Now, wait, let me think . . . curse . . . , curse . . . no, so far no curses, just ordinary mistakes.

One day I got a phone call from my daughter with the news that there were two poles by her front door with doll heads on them. She was an art school student and unfortunately the neighborhood where she lived was what most moms would call borderline safe. Borderline safe is suburban lingo for: something might happen but if it does it won't be too terrible. Her next-door neighbor explained that the doll heads were voodoo dolls. One of them had her very recognizable hair style. Should she move? Should she stay? My mind was immediately racing for an answer. I said something like, "Put a big cross and a Jewish Star on your door and get out of there as fast as you can." How do I handle this? She is living in America, in the 'burbs'—this shouldn't be happening.

I called a friend who was a Pastor near her neighborhood. He told me that tribal beliefs, spells and witchcraft were rampant in her part of town. He said an enterprising individual could earn a living driving residents from her neighborhood to the Root Man in North Florida. The Root Man? Why didn't I think of that? Wait a minute, I live in North Florida. Is this where the Root Man lives? Only the dolls know for sure.

What's Gat You're Chewing?

To start the day off right, yesterday I stopped at a local coffee shop before work. I ordered a small coffee and a butter croissant. The clerk couldn't swipe my card. I couldn't remember my zip code. My croissant order was overlooked, and I spilled my coffee. I had thirty minutes left so I played it safe and sat in my car. If you are waiting for work, the bus, the train, or Godot, it's a perfect opportunity to think about the world, places far away, and other people's problems.

I sat and thought about a book I just finished reading. Writers are readers and I just finished reading the biography of an American journalist in X land. To be politically correct, I will not reveal the name of the country. In X it is commonplace for everyone to spend four to six hours a day chewing a leaf called gat. Gat is a narcotic leaf. Everyone chews gat. In the middle of the workday, journalists leave the office for four-hour-long gat breaks. Housewives, the butcher, the baker, the candlestick maker, everyone in X chews gat. The solution to coming down from the gat high is to chew more gat.

Much to my surprise, someone suggested that I consider the American coffee habit and not be so judgmental. Okay, being a fair-minded person, I looked objectively at my own coffee habit, and it is not the same as chewing gat. I drink coffee and then I

> *I looked objectively at my own coffee habit, and it is not the same as chewing gat.*

go to work. Housewives, if there are any left, drink coffee and still do the laundry. Drinking coffee may be addictive but it is not debilitating.

The American journalist reported that she never saw anyone in the country of X reading a book, and that there is a very high poverty rate in X. The truth is, I have not seen anyone here reading a book either. I am going to take a radical risk and connect the dots between their national habit of gat chewing, high illiteracy, and poverty. Does it matter which came first? Reading is essential for day-to-day living. The mothers in X can't read so they dilute and misuse the formula for their babies. I am not sure how the author could have been working for a newspaper as a journalist if no one in X can read, but the fact remains that illiteracy, poverty and gat chewing are rampant.

There are twenty-four hours in a day and if half of the waking time is spent chewing or recovering from chewing gat then there is not a whole lot of time left for, dare I say it—work or reading. The solution? "Think, Miss Pat *think*." I don't have one. Solving international problems is out of my jurisdiction. I drink coffee and I go to work after stopping at the abovementioned coffee shop. "Anything else?" Well, I am grateful that I was born here and not there, that my problems are small and that I can read books about gat instead of chewing it. As for my addictions, my coffee habit is manageable. Usually.

ONCE UPON A TIME

There was a time when I went to my local library every week to check out Story Boxes. It was a happy time. I was the storyteller on our local TV station and at area preschools. Each box had a book with an accompanying puppet. The puppet provided an interactive element that could be used to promote the theme of the book. Not anymore. When I returned to the library for some storytelling, I found fewer boxes and where are the puppets? One box had a stuffed whale, another had a bird with a book warning not to cut down trees. Why do I have a problem with all of this? Am I in favor of killing whales or robbing birds of a place to build a nest? No. But I am also in favor of giving big problems to adults and giving children—child size problems, like what happens if you kiss a frog or try to ski on spaghetti. (*More Spaghetti I Say*, by Rita Golden Gelman).

Is 'Once upon a time' a thing of the past? What about, 'And they lived happily ever after.'? That one is definitely fiction. The good news is that children still like to sing silly songs, march around the room and to quote a poster that I saw in one preschool, "What if the Hokey Pokey *is* what it is all about . . ."

Although I was discouraged by the lack of Story Boxes, all was not lost. I spied a book that I hadn't seen in over twenty years, *The Boy Who Fed His Fish*

What if the Hokey Pokey is what it is all about . . ."

Too Much by Hap Palmer. This book embraces all that is good in early childhood literature. A boy messes up and feeds his pet fish too much. What will happen? He has been warned by the pet shop owner, Mr. A. Carp that if he feeds Otto too much something will happen. What happens? His fish grows, and grows, until finally it has outgrown the family bathtub and needs to be hauled to the town pool. In the midst of the confusion, the police and the firemen are called. They are more than willing to come and help. Instead of saying "Look kid your fish is going to *die*, they respond with, "What! A boy has fed his fish too much! We'll come right away." I love it.

Let's apply this to adult life. What! A girl has spent too much! We'll come right away. If I overspend my bank account (something that never happens), it will grow and grow and grow until finally I have to take all of the money out because it just won't fit! The bank is too small. What! A man has had too much to drink! We'll come right away. Long past sober and surrounded by empty bottles we find Hector alert and doing calculus! The more he drinks the smarter he gets! What! I have eaten too much! The more I eat, the thinner I get. I am more athletic with every mouthful. If you haven't already guessed, my unsolicited advice is to climb the bean stalk, marry the prince, and—ski on spaghetti.

April Showers Bring

May is the month we associate with flowers and a big thank you goes out to the month of April, but in Florida, I think it only rained once. We use flowers in interesting ways. They are used to decorate both weddings and funerals. We give them to sick people. They brighten up a room and enhance a dinner table. People have probably been picking flowers for as long as there have been flowers.

I recently read *The Scent of Scandal* which documents a true crisis over an illegal orchid. Fifteen years ago, this scandal almost brought down the botanical garden in my hometown. Illegal orchid? Yes. You cannot just pick and bring home. There are international laws protecting native plants. The book was interesting. I learned that there is an orchid cult which is cutthroat, dark and deceitful. Good grief! I have met collectors and I have met hoarders. But orchids? A flower? *Nature*? There is something indecent about it. Hording belongs with materialism and not nature.

I learned that serious orchid collectors can be strange and well . . . crazy. There is a point when a person crosses the line from gardening to nuts. How does this happen? Once again, my answer is, I have no idea. However, if your name is Rose, or Lily, Heather, Violet, or Daisy, beware. The obsessed collectors are

I learned that serious orchid collectors can be strange and well ... crazy.

out there and who knows, they may come after you.

By typing 'Flowers' into a Google Search, I was able to do some scholarly research and found one possible answer to the why and how of this floral travesty. Our human need to analyze and categorize has led to the assignment of a flower for each month, like the monthly birth stone. It is also possible to go online and find a personality trait associated with each flower. One example is the flowering anemone. Never heard of it? Possibly because it means 'fading hope.' Orchids on the other hand, are associated with such alluring adjectives as 'refinement' and 'femininity.' We may be on to something here. No one is hording, stealing and black marking the hopeless anemone. It is possible, in fact it is an undeniable truth that the orchid flower itself is responsible for the scandalous theft due to its irresistible allure. (Where was I when the orchid thieves needed a defense lawyer?)

The Botanical Garden scandalized by the orchid crisis, recently petitioned for a zoning change to build a restaurant. It would be a Sky Garden with a parking garage to accommodate the crowd who will flock to enjoy an expensive meal with a beautiful view. Always one to do some soul searching, I wonder if I would I eat there. Probably, I like posh and my ethical standards diminish every year. That said, and with moderation in mind, I encourage you to look up the flower assigned to your birth month. My birth flower is Lily of the Valley. It means 'increased happiness.' Definitely better than fading hope.

The Right to Bare Arms

Beware, this is political. Elections have given me a chance to reflect on our freedoms. In keeping with my air head image, I will first explore the freedoms that lack significance, and then those which may be significantly lacking. America is 'The Land of the Free and the Brave.' We are free to brave short sleeves, sleeveless, and halter tops. You may be frowned on, but you will not be arrested. In America for the most part, what we wear is a choice. The basic rule is to be wearing something in the basic places most of the time.

In America, being female, I am free to go where I want, and when I want but this is not true globally. Just to get a glimpse of how twisted a reality that is, try to imagine the situation with gender reversal. Imagine a country where the men are not allowed to go outside alone or drive a car. They have to walk around covered up except for their eyes. They are just too desirable they must be hidden or else who knows what might happen.

Elections have given me a chance to reflect on our freedoms.

Worldwide not everyone is free to marry the person of their choice. The global Westernization of the world is changing the tradition of family arranged marriages, but I was surprised to read that it is still a popular practice. It is true that non-arranged marriages have not been working out too well, but it is a freedom. One study reported that almost half of the world's marriages are prearranged. Thinking back, who in your social arena would your parents have contracted for you to marry? A scary thought? It is my understanding that in arranged marriages men have the right of refusal. They are given choices to visit and then accept or reject, similar to purchasing real estate.

Another choice we should not take for granted is the right to determine the number of children we will have. Recently, an Illinois couple celebrated the birth of their 100th grandchild. Leo & Ruth Zanger have 53 grandchildren, 46 great grandchildren and one great-great grandchild. "There is always room for one more," Ruth happily quips. You can do that in America. It's one freedom we don't often talk about, but it is important.

Let me see, what other personal freedoms do we have? I can eat what I want, but that is pretty standard world-wide, except for the forbidden pig, or cow depending on how far east you travel. In countries that reject certain foods, I don't think it is an issue that results in arrest, except for the consumption of alcohol. Remember prohibition? I hope you can't remember prohibition, no one that old should be alive and reading this. My parents were a part of the 'speakeasy' generation.

Did you think that this was going to be about gun control? I hesitate to go there. In America we are free to defend ourselves and own a gun. I thought that was what the police were for. Why is it always my team, the Christian Right, that advocate owning guns for protection? I thought that was what God was for. Now, let me see, I have covered dress, food, marriage, childbirth, guns, religion—Oh! How could I forget? The freedom to print your opinion.

Treat Or Treat

It's tricky to be anti-Halloween. "What! What is wrong with you Miss Pat? Are you against candy? Do you hate little children? They look so cute in their costumes." Yes, they do and when I step on a scale there is no question that I approve of candy. Why celebrate a holiday that features death and ugliness? I am the equivalent of scrooge at Christmas when it comes to Halloween. It is not as if we are decorating our homes with flowers. We are decorating with cute little tarantulas, skeletons, and witches. If I am not mistaken the keyword is 'Boo' as in "I will frighten you."

I did celebrate Halloween when I was a child, and it was an adventurous holiday for children only. Grown-ups were merely the chaperones that guided us through the neighborhood. They did not run around dressed up in costumes. Dracula? Blood dripping from fake scars? I just am not for it. Do I hear a chorus of "Lighten up, it's just for fun?" No thank you. Not interested.

*By October, fall is really here. Well, not **here**, because I am in Florida, and it is still ninety degrees.*

I *am* for celebrating the fall season and by October, fall is really here. Well, not really here, because I am in Florida and it is still ninety degrees, but it is somewhere and I have memories of crisp fall air, apples, apples and more apples. Being the humble Queen of homemade applesauce, I am all about the fall season. The only boo in my October is a boohoo because I have no leaves to shuffle through and the air is not crisp. However, I will not be negative, not me, I may slam Halloween, but I will enjoy a pumpkin latte, and suggest that we change Trick or Treat to Treat or Treat. With Treat or Treat in mind, I'll have a slice of apple pie with my pumpkin latte.

The Lone Ranger

I don't want to startle anyone but what I am about to share is a little startling. My nephew went to a new dentist and the dentist cleaned his teeth. No hygienist, no dental assistant, this dentist cleaned my nephew's teeth, all by himself. This is almost as surprising as a doctor making what use to be called 'house calls' or having a home office. House calls were even before my generation. The rationale behind that ancient practice is that the patient is sick and needs to stay home and rest; the doctor is well so he should be the one who goes out and visits the sick person. Crazy, no?

My parents took me to a doctor whose office was in his home. It was before everyone was a specialist. You could have anything wrong from an earache to a heart attack and this one man would help you. It was based on the theory that he knew medicine and understood how the human body worked.

Although life is complicated and teams are often essential, I just can't get with the team mind set. When my daughter was in middle school, she wanted to play soccer. She presented a stellar argument with two key facts. She wanted to run in a large open field. She wanted to play on a team. I play singles tennis. I want to stand in a clearly defined rectangle enclosed by a wire fence and I want to face my opponent one on one.

The clinic approach to medicine, and dentistry are examples of the team mindset that has replaced the persona of the strong individual. Realtors now work in teams, architects work in teams, even teachers frequently have assistants. Have people become less capable? Probably, but it is also a product of big business and the complexity we have experienced since technology has come to help us simplify.

Let's look at teaching. Yes, one teacher could do it if they have nerves of steel and only need about four hours of sleep a night. Parents are no longer there to support them, and neither is the principal. I am quoting a woman that I met recently who chose to leave the field of education. She was a high school English teacher; and she now cleans teeth. She cleans my teeth. I am not knocking dental hygienists, I depend on them for my ability to chew, but it takes a lot to become a licensed teacher and to walk away from years of training, certifying, and credentialing, I would call it a drastic decision. To be fair, I have also met people who have left the corporate world to become teachers, so I guess the answer is that no one really knows what they want to be doing.

I found my niche in preschool. Are you surprised? The rhymes, the songs, the adorable children with big bows or wearing spider man shirts and carrying Thomas lunch boxes. I fit right in. Preschool was my happy place. I enjoy using words that rhyme. Far be it from me to brag, but I am famous for such quotable phrases as, "I rhyme all the time." Although it is hard to call a three-year-old a student, I used to write down the cute things my students said. Sitting at the lunch table, one little girl told her friend, "Don't talk with your mouth open." Excellent advice. I make that mistake all the time.

Roses Are Red—
Violets Are Black

Am I being redundant when I say, "I love Valentine's Day"? The history behind Valentine's Day is a little sketchy but does it matter? Who can be against love? I looked it up and all this affection began in the third century when the Roman Emperor Claudis II assassinated two men named Valentine. The Romans did a lot of assassinating and a lot of wild debauchery. I am glad that we've said goodbye to ancient Rome and hello to Western Romanticism and Capitalism and who will admit to being anti-love? More important—who doesn't like chocolate?

Is it because I am hard to please, that love seems to be everywhere, and I am out of step? I heard a woman on TV say that she loved her sheets. She looked so happy. I have already accepted that my love level is smaller than that of the couple who love their bathroom now that a new tub has been fitted over the old one, but sheets? What's wrong with me?

Valentine's Day can bring out the best in all of us. I like to send Valentine cards and I sent my cards early this year. Real cards, especially Valentine's Day cards are one of life's simple pleasures that enable us to show how much we care and to show off our true loving dispositions. Simply put, I will destroy anyone who tries to take sending cards from me.

Always more than willing to show off my DIY skill set, like to make my own Valentine's Day candy. I melt chocolate in a microwave and then pour it into mini heart molds. Does it get any easier? Using a paper lace doily, I present my chocolate hearts for the world to admire. "Oooh you *made* these?" I respond with a modest smile, thinking, well yeah, it was one step beyond opening a bag and dumping candy into a bowl. "Yes, I do make my own Valentine's Day candy. Why scrimp when it comes to showing how much you care."

Unfortunately, Valentine's Day also brings up the topic of fake affection. Fake affection is everywhere and it deserves extreme banning. I was recently reminded of a clip from the 2006 movie *Idiocracy*. *Idiocracy* spoofed what we now live with. In one scene, a department store Greeter was giving shoppers a hug and saying, "I love you." I thought it was very funny until I was waiting to get into a restaurant and the line monitor/greeter was hugging the patrons to redirect any grumbling, trouble, or boredom. Cooing, "Hey honey—how you doin' darling?" She hugged her way down the line. My look probably said it all, and she hugged the woman behind me.

Fake affection is everywhere, and it deserves extreme banning.

Next on my Don't Do It list is the clerk who calls me 'Honey' or 'Dear.' Am I against someone saying a simple, "Thank you, dear?" You bet. My attitude is—I don't know you, you don't know me, why the term of endearment? All I did was give you $1.00 for gum. It's very confusing. "But Miss Pat what about love? I saw on Facebook that someone heard you use the word 'hate'. What about Valentine's Day and your cheery disposition?" Oh. Okay. Happy Valentine's Day. "Nope, not good enough." Happy Valentine's Day to the people I like. "More, take a deep breath." Happy Valentine's Day to the people I don't like. "I knew you could do it! Here, have a chocolate heart, I made them myself."

Yummy Art

I live in a town that prides itself on its culture. There is a highbrow approach to art and life. I have a reasonably highbrow and I enjoy visiting my local art museum. The museum was founded by John Ringling, the owner of The Ringling Brothers Circus. To define himself as a man of taste beyond clowns and elephants, Mr. Ringling collected highbrow art. He chose the art of painter John Paul Rubens and his collection of Rubens is the foundation for our local art museum. The paintings are not just big; they are colossal in size. One painting, The Sabine Women is 16 feet high and 20 feet wide. The rape of the Sabine women is an odd topic because most of the Rubens have a religious theme.

Scattered among the religious Rubens are classic still life paintings. If you ask the average American, myself included, what type of painting is a 'still life,' most people will tell you that 'still life' is a bowl of fruit, or a vase with flowers and a bowl of fruit, or maybe some veggies and a bowl of fruit. Not so. The original use of the term 'still life' meant dead. Definitely still. Before the animal rights movement, artists happily painted dead pheasants draped across a table, or perhaps a shot duck, now brought inside and arranged with care on a slab of marble. Dare I say, I don't like it. I guess I was not meant to be an art connoisseur or museum critic. I am too critical. Because art is everywhere and not just in the art museum, I recently applied my critical nature to critique kitchen art.

Kitchen art is unique because it is different than what people have in the rest of the house. Poultry reign supreme in kitchen art and recently I saw a perfect example. Beautifully mounted and framed were two lithographs of a hen and a rooster. Picture #1 Mr. Rooster is on the left, mom hen is on the right. Picture #2 Mom hen is on the left, and daddy rooster is on the right. This is very exciting. The proud poultry are well represented, with details and shading that evoke images of eggs rather than how great you look before being battered and fried.

Kitchen art is unique because it is usually different than what people have in the rest of the house.

Ducks are a popular subject for Long Island and New England kitchen art. Mallard ducks deck the walls of East Hampton kitchens. Kitchen art is used to enhance Country Kitchen décor, a style which is not 'the farm' but the farmer's market. The microwave is tastefully hidden. There is no black, or chrome. The emphasis is rustic, but not so rustic as to be authentic. This is not the kitchen where we slaughter hens, or better put it is not the kitchen where we handle newly slaughtered hens by removing the feathers. This is where we make them into a yummy meal using fresh ingredients, herbs and spices. Enhanced with baskets, not too many, just one here and one there, add at least one piece of copper cookware, a dash of blue and white china, a few wooden spoons, a large whisk and what you have is a look that is warm, delicious, and what time is dinner?

WORD FOR WORD

What's Happening to Words?

"What's happening to words?" Crabby me asks. Words are being given new definitions that challenge the very print on a dictionary page. If you are under the age of fifty, you may as well stop reading now. This is a 'senior' rant. It will seem crabby, crabby, crabby. For some reason the little things that are not even noticed by younger folks jump out at Medicare card holders with ferocity. Is it that we have too much free time? Is it pent up frustration that needs a release? A lack of vitamin C, D or E? I have a friend who likes to say, "Who knows?" Someone else might ask, "Who cares?" Being a writer, I care because I have a protective interest in words. I love words. They are the music notes of writing. So, don't mess with my words or the definitions that I know and trust.

> *Don't mess with my words or the definitions that I know and trust.*

Who is responsible for altering the definition of the word 'final'? Final used to mean 'the end', last, over, no more, done. 'Final' has been given a new twenty-first century definition. Final has been redefined to mean, 'I will continue to harass you until you comply.'

Example #1: My recent experience entering a well-known sweepstakes. For weeks I have been getting a series of Final Notice emails to motivate me to complete the endless entry form I started in a moment of folly and leisure. What part of 'final' do they not understand? Didn't they give me my last chance two weeks ago? Wasn't that the final opportunity to waste my time?

Example #2: I experienced a similar disregard for the word 'final' when my cute little car turned three and crossed the 30,000-mile threshold into automotive doom. I was not to worry because I could extend my extended warranty with any one of the companies that sent numerous notices in the mail claiming to be The Final Notice. One postal notice even included a sample bill with projected repair expenses. The total was more than the value of my car. Not only did I get notices in the mail; I received a series of Final Notice phone calls. Did I crumble under such pressure? I DID NOT. That was 30,000 miles ago and now at 66,000 my car is still running, no repairs needed.

I like my car a lot. I wash it, well, I should clarify, I get it washed. I keep the inside clean.

One of the features that I enjoy the most is OnStar. I love having OnStar. OnStar is perfect for the person who cannot use a GPS and drive. Yes, that person exists, I know her well, she considers it to be impossible multi-tasking. Unfortunately, OnStar has joined the plot to eradicate words that in any way represent closure. "Do you want to end directions?"

asks the robot. I naively respond with "Yes." "Yes" is not good enough, clarification is needed. I am asked again. "Do you want to cancel directions?" "Yes," I scream. I am verbally abusive to machinery.

'Final' now means something akin to 'forever.' When I get a Final Notice, it no longer ushers in a conclusion. Everything that used to end, no longer stops but joins a continuing line of progressive notices, reminders, mailings and phone calls. I call the trend CPMD, Continual Progression Mentality Disorder.

The Mom

I sent my son an email and signed it 'The Mom.' I am easily influenced by the success of others. Do you remember 'The Donald'? Following an interview with the first Mrs. Trump, eyebrows were raised at her use of the article THE before saying Donald's name. The simple addition of three letters can skyrocket a person from ordinary to royal faster than a speeding pen. Obviously, I am not aspiring for the Presidency but maybe by adding THE to my title of 'Mom' I can lift the status a little higher. Why hasn't somebody done this sooner?

Grammatically speaking THE is an article. Not only is THE an article, it is a *definite* article which elevates it to its current status of distinguishing The Donald from just any ole' Donald. I am not ready for The Patricia, but The Mom sounds pretty good. If I were answering the phone for a business, I could test this theory. "Bob, you have a call from The Michael." Obviously, last names can be added to avoid confusion. "Bob, you have a call

> *The simple addition of three letters can skyrocket a person from ordinary to royal faster than a speeding pen.*

from The Michael Jones." Now Michael has risen to the status of a European with a Title. The Count, The Prince, or in the colonies we say, The Most Honorable Judge.

This is all part of what I humbly call The Prefix Paradigm. Names alone do not supply enough information. We want to know if the caller is male, female, single, married, and how high up the education ladder have they gone. How do you find all of this out in one simple sentence? Look at the prefix. Just a few letters can supply the information we need to organize, clarify and categorize.

In this age of universality shouldn't all occupations be given a boost? In addition to The Mom, I am recommending that THE be used before occupations. For example: The Baker Charles. The Accountant Edward. The Surfer John. The highly coveted prefix Dr. before a name, be it medical or scholarly, cannot be ignored. If you want to offend, and I try to suppress the urge, call anyone with a Dr. before their name 'Mr.' This offends both the medical profession and those in academia who long for the status of the medical profession.

The Prefix Paradigm is taken to the max in the military by adding a person's rank before their name and using 'Sir' to designate those who are above the ordinary enlisted 'private.' There are parents that insist on having their children say, "Yes Sir" and "No Ma'am" which makes me wonder if they are not mini-military strong holds in disguise. In closing, I want to thank The Donald for his positive contribution to American family life. Thank you for setting a precedent that enables me to replace 'Ma' with The Mom.

Write or Wrong?

I don't speak. All I do is write. If you are sitting next to me, I'll hand you a note. My rationale is that it gives people a chance to think before they respond. I do run the risk of having them think I'm nuts, but every positive has a negative or something like that. What if no one spoke and we all just wrote? What a quiet world! What a great world if the only sounds were the sounds in nature. What a not-so-great world if you live in a city, then you would have just city sounds like the subway. Now there's a thought; New York City void of all human speech, only machine noises—cars, tires, horns, subways. It might be nice. Robbery would go down, and muggings would be less frequent. A tap on the shoulder and someone hands you a note, "Your money or your life." They can't spell, it says, "Your meny or your wife." You're confused; you don't have a wife. The whole thing is taking way too long, but you can't call out for help. He has a gun. He shoots.

What if no one spoke and we all just wrote?

I wonder whatever happened to handwriting analysis. For that matter, whatever happened to handwriting? I heard a rumor that they are no longer teaching cursive writing in schools. Truly, the beginning of the end. Everyone wants to print because they don't need to write, they just use their electronic devices and why waste the paper? Not to date myself (no one else is, so why not?), in elementary school I used pens that had a little lever that sucked up the ink. I have enough self-control not to be a hoarder but if I were a hoarder, I would hoard pens. A hoarder with focus is called a Collector. From Parker to Bic, I love them all, such limitless design and style. Antique dealers have collections of fountain pens, but the shape and design are, to my untrained eye, all too similar. Somewhere in the industrial mass production of everything, pens got style. If you doubt the accuracy of this bold statement just stand in front of the pen display at any office supply store. A true tribute to human creativity, second only to shoes, and purses.

Let's move on to pen's partner—Paper. I don't dare say this in front of everyone for fear of being labeled as non-environmentally caring; but I am passionate about paper. I love, love, love paper. I do love trees and I thank them because paper is so great. I am not anti-environment. I am for moderation, the responsible use of trees for paper and well . . . for wood. A healthy restriction on the production of paper products, will enable us to welcome, cherish and appreciate cards, books, and gift wrap. Here are a few of my suggestions for paper conservation.

1. Keep people like me out of the school copy room. I am ashamed. I admit it. The machine has a power of its own and when I want 10 copies, I get 100 and then it won't stop and now there are 1000 but the format is wrong, so I have to do it again.

2. All bills, notices, and final statements need to be eliminated. Waste. Waste. Waste. What a waste.

3. Advertising via mail needs to be banned. Simply put, "Don't call us, we'll call you," unless you have coupons.

I miss stationary shops with shelves of colored paper and rows of creative cards. I don't want email greetings. I want a card I can hold, open and save in a real box that has a latch and not a click.

Babble Works

I spoil my cats. My children are grown so Simon and Brina are the daily recipients of lovingly displaced neurotic concern. I give them my best maternal attention and the focus is none other than, my all-time favorite, FOOD. A respected TV chef is now making cat food. My Sabrina loves, loves, loves her chicken with gravy. Why do I have a problem with this? Celebrities and celebrity chefs have always had products lines.

Products and fame go hand and hand. For years I have happily bought a well-known Hollywood star's salad dressing. Does the younger generation know or care that the man on the label was an actor? I also own a pressure cooker and enjoy coffee that has a famous chef's face on the label. He didn't develop the pressure cooker that carries his name, or the coffee. It is more of an endorsement. Did the famous actor make the salad dressing? This is getting very confusing.

What's wrong with a chef making pet food? I will declare to a highly select group of readers, that a chef shouldn't cross the line from making people food to pet food. She has crossed the line. To switch from people food to making cat food makes me say "Yuck." There, I've said it. Kitty and pup may love table scraps but boldly I ask, "Do you cook for pets or for people? Honey, it was a poor decision on all counts."

That said, what about food product names? Let's look. What's in a name? Was Aunt Jemima real? If you have pondered the authenticity of Aunt Jemima and Uncle Ben, there is a 'tell all' website that does just that, it tells us if they were real or not. As for the beloved pancake auntie, she's a fake. Aunt Jemima was developed in 1889 by the CEOs of the Pearl Melly Company. If you are wondering about Uncle Ben, he too was a marketing scheme that worked. We know Mrs. Smith (pies) isn't real and a big thank you goes out to the late Andy Rooney for debunking that scandalous fraud. Was Betty Crocker a real person? Did I hear someone say, "Who cares?"

What's in a name?

I love the story behind Birdseye frozen vegetables. There was a real Mr. Birdseye, a Brooklyn taxidermist who saw fish successfully frozen in the natural world and with a seven-dollar investment of a fan, some ice and brine, he developed a product called frozen food. He sold the patent in 1927 for twenty-two million dollars. Why can't I think of something like that? He went on to invent a harpoon for whales which raises the question, "Were people still harpooning whales in the 1920's?" That seems sort of primitive.

Inspired by Mr. Birdseye's success, have you seen my foolproof, Catch Your Run-Away Cat trap? Inside a box lined with cat nip, I have recorded the sound of a can of cat food being opened, which for some reason may be preferable to walking outside and opening numerous cans of cat food in the hope that your precious darling will hear the familiar snap and come running. The patent is 'in process.'

The last product name that I will scrutinize is Haagen-Dazs ice cream. In 1976 a man sat at his kitchen table uttering syllables that he liked the sound of and came up with two words that mean absolutely nothing. They are not Danish, they are not anything, but they are two words that Mr. Reuben Mattus, a marketing genius, knew would sell ice cream. They were Haagen-Dazs. Next came the explanation that the name was inspired by the Danish treatment of Jews in WW2. Obviously, this explanation is after the fact. If this was an attempt to honor Denmark, we would be eating Copenhagen Cream, not Haagen Dazs. According to Reuben's daughter Doris, her father "Sat at the kitchen table for hours saying nonsensical words until he came up with a combination he liked." I can relate to this. My son calls me Dobro. After the fact, he discovered that a dobro is a musical instrument like a dulcimer. He liked the sound of the word. Haagen Dazs has outsold brands with real names proving that babble works.

Bumper Sticker Readings $5.00

I love bumper stickers, but I have walked around my car three times and I still can't find a bumper. Even without a bumper, bumper stickers make for interesting reading. The COEXIST slogan peace sticker has had its final hurrah. Usually sharing the road with: I EAT VEGETABLES and I LOVE YOGA it was clever, but it is now definitely passé.

Not to take a snob-like attitude, I sometimes wonder about people. Recently, I was waiting at a red light in line behind EAT FRUIT and I LOVE MY CAT. What can I say? I eat fruit. I love my cat. I am not sure if I am willing to publicize such personal and revealing information. Right now, and in fact always, I have nothing glued onto my car that describes my life, my interests, or my shopping habits.

Even without a bumper, bumper stickers make for interesting reading.

Being naughty but nice, I humbly offer suggestions for new bumper stickers:

I Love My Salamander

Peanuts Give Me Hives

- Coffee Drinker—Warning: Frequent Stops

- God, Guns & Gum (This one has a picture of a gun covered with chewed pink bubble gum. God is laughing in the background.)

- If You Can't Read This—Then You Are Too Far Away.

Recently, I was on the road behind a car with a bumper sticker that admonished drivers to CHOOSE CIVILITY. I have to comment. Let's take a closer look at CHOOSE CIVILITY. Because I watch the news, I know for a fact that few people understand the word 'Civility'. Choose Civility over what? Barbarism? Cannibalism? Patriotism? We know it has to be an 'ism.' Be more specific please, the schoolteacher in me does not approve.

One bumper sticker really jarred my thinking. I pulled into a parking spot, (I have always been proud of my ability to parallel park) behind a driver who claimed to be a geometric shape. Their bumper sticker bragged: I Am a (shape of a square). Excuse me, but this one must be called out for a critique. It's okay to self-identify with a geometric shape but why 'square'? Although I am possibly out of touch with personal reality, I consider myself to be a diamond or a circle or a heart. I like to flatter myself with positive adjectives such as: stylish, loving, and why would I advertise anything less? Since the term 'square' went out with cassette tapes, this driver is probably over ninety. My response is: "Why are you still driving?"

I admire people who advertise products and services on the back window of their cars. I never have a pen handy, but I am impressed with their marketing savvy. For those readers who remember the Western series *Gunsmoke* and Paladin, I will share my car window marketing slogan.

Miss Pat—Have Humor—Won't Travel.

Bumper stickers and car advertising are not the only opportunities to read while driving. Signs are everywhere. I am not referring to the over-abundance of store and business signage; but the signs that the DOT has set along the road to gently guide me, warn me, and mold me into a better person. One day I decided to count the DOT signs from one intersection to my destination. The distance was less than a quarter of a mile. I counted thirty signs. Some were on the left, some were on the right, I was welcomed, directed, warned, and distracted. I will take one giant leap of faith and say I could have gotten there without all the help.

Feel the Beat

In my nonathletic mind, exercise and music go together. Jazzercize, Sweatin' to the Oldies, Zumba. There is something special about moving to music, even if you are out of step, the last one to turn, and facing the wrong side of the room when the music stops. My current Zumba class is multi-cultural and fun.

Do I cringe when my Zumba teacher happily sings out, "Move your ass"? Not 21st century me. Acceptable language has changed, especially with the "F" word now taking center stage. I should preface this by saying that I grew up in a house where 'shut up' was called a 'bad' word.

In Arizona, I joined a Zumba class that was rigorous, rigorous, rigorous. What a workout! The instructor bragged that she had trained people to dance with Disney. Mickey? I don't want to dance with the Mouse; I just want to enjoy myself and get closer to the word 'fit.'

My best dance class experience was in Florida. One day, I happened to be strolling by a park and an African dance troupe was performing on the park stage. They were amazing. Just when you thought that they couldn't possibly do more, they would spring back to life and out do themselves. I got their contact information and was invited to join them for their weekly practice at a nearby community center.

The practice routine was fun, but the best part happened at the close of each session. When the pattern of dance moves was over, we had an opportunity to create our own dance to the beat of live drummers. Inside a circle of pulsating fellow dancers, one at a time, the brave could step into the circle and 'show their stuff.' I think I did an impressive job for being the only (is it okay to say *white?*) woman in the group. I am convinced that the world would be a happier place if daily we danced to the beat of live drumming. My advice? Throw out the medicine, get off the couch and "Move your . . . ."

> *I am convinced that the world would be a happier place if daily we danced to the beat of live drumming.*

Proverbial Wisdom

I enjoy retirement and the time it gives me to research important and meaningless topics. I spend a lot of time on my computer exploring and recently went down the 'proverb' internet trail. Proverbs in the Bible are a pleasure to read, however proverbs outside of the Bible, along with metaphors, parable-type statements and directions on the Stove Top box leave me scratching my head. Proverbs are a category of literature, the analysis of which has been ignored long enough. Looking up the word 'Proverb,' I learned that a proverb is a short pithy saying. Pithy? Next, I looked up the word 'pithy.' Pithy: full of pith. Better informed, I will move forward.

Proverbs are a category of literature, the analysis of which has been ignored long enough.

A lot of proverbial expressions are inaccurately attributed to the Bible. Some people are disappointed to learn that 'God helps those that help themselves' is not in the Bible. This popular expression was not penned by Moses or David but by our very own Ben Franklin. I welcome this as good news because I don't really want to have Divine Assistance be based on my self-help performance. Ben Franklin, on the other hand, was an accomplished individual, someone who could smile at his self-help accomplishments—electricity and so forth. Good job, Ben.

Growing up, I often heard the expression, 'Into each life some rain must fall.' When I moved to Florida, I purchased knee high rain boots, a very stylish raincoat, and a large sturdy umbrella. It rained a lot. When I went to the Arizona desert, I wondered if my life would improve. There was very little rain. Was life any better? One day the temperature hit 108 degrees. Not to appear shallow and ignorant of proverbial wisdom, all I can say is that it was very hot.

Another proverb, 'Don't throw the baby out with the bath water,' always stumped me. I heard it a lot in my parent's house, I would nod and smile pretending to get it. This one still stretches my brain. 'Don't throw the baby out with the bathwater.' Think. The bathwater cleans the baby, when the process is done the baby is clean and the water is dirty, you throw out the water, you keep the clean baby. *Think*. It helps to substitute other words in the same pattern when trying to understand a proverb. If you are cutting the lawn don't throw the grass out with the lawnmower. You don't throw out the lawn mower. If you are washing dishes, don't throw the dishes away when done. Absolutely not, that would be a big mistake.

The writing of proverbs seems to have stopped around the turn of the 19th century. Needless to say, I will attempt to fill the void.

- Don't take a bath after a shower.

- Bite the sandwich but leave the crust. (They're starting to flow.)

- Don't wash a car that won't start.

Yes, well, I think that I know why the writing of proverbs is a lost art. My short attention span has kicked in, so I will now explore other forms of non-conventional writing. Shall we scrutinize the Haiku and the, oh-so-literary, limerick? Haiku is an interesting poetic style, and so are limericks. Unfortunately, limericks are associated with drunk Irish people which stirs my native blood a little. Not a lot, just a little. Haiku are associated with sensitivity and thought. Could these be representative of cultural differences? Let's reverse the cultures. What would a Japanese limerick look like? "There once was a maid from Tokyo . . . " And now, an Irish Haiku: "Ice floating in a glass of clear liquid."

Let's take a closer look at Haiku. The definition of Haiku is: Japanese poetry that embraces two images with a word that joins them in a very sensitive, creative and somewhat boring manner. Next, let's delve deeper into the classic Limerick. Limerick is named after a town in Ireland, and it is a short often obscene rhyme sung or chanted in bars by my ancestors. Questions flood my creative mind. Could someone, namely me, translate Dante's Inferno into limerick form? Should I google Beowulf? Did Shakespeare visit Ireland? The possibilities seem endless, so many opportunities for research and study! Wait. Stop. Should I be doing this? What does Proverbial Wisdom say? If the Shoe Fits Wear It. When In Rome, Do as the Romans Do. A Bird in the Hand Is Worth Two in the Bush. I will pick one. I pick, I pick . . . Better Late Than Never.

DIFFERENT STROKES FOR DIFFERENT FOLKS

I am a picky reader. A picky reader is not unlike a picky eater. Who wants to eat everything? Do I chow down on fast food? I like steak. Driving past a popular Taco eatery, I noticed the sign COME IN FOR OUR NEW STEAK MENU. Is it steak or is it a taco? Because I am a picky reader, on my last visit to the library I confidently checked out a biography of William Faulkner. Harmless, right? Page thirty had a graphic description of a man being burned alive. In the past, I considered looking in the YA, Young Adult section for books to fit my picky palette. "Lordy" (to quote a friend from Georgia) witches, ghouls, the occult. What's left? I love children's books, but I want something that takes longer than three minutes to read.

Let's face it, books are out, videos are in, books take too long to read, and it all fits perfectly with my being a writer. Yes, I would choose to write when people have stopped reading. Makes sense. Fits the pattern. At my last visit to the library, the staff looked so lonely and bored, just sitting there waiting, waiting . . . Hmmm, maybe I should write novels. Defying all odds, I will switch from short humor to writing novels. How about *The Readers of the Lost Art*? Armed with my catchy title, I will start. I will be inspired by the great novelists of the past. Did Tolstoy write *War and Peace* in long hand, or did he use a typewriter?

A daughter of the sixties, I have always liked the expression Different Strokes for Different Folks. Because I like to keep things simple, I use only one or two cliches to guide me through the hills and valleys of life. Different Strokes for Different Folks is at the top of a short list that enables me to justify all kinds of behavior, personal and otherwise. When confronted with people and situations that could be labeled weird or radical instead of responding with a shocked "Why are you doing *that*?" I am able to say, "Oh. You ride a cheetah to town? Well, different strokes for different folks. I take the bus."

> *Did Tolstoy write* **War and Peace** *in long hand, or did he use a typewriter?*

Different writers have varying approaches to the craft of writing. I like to apply the Different Stokes mantra to my writing style. Many, if not most, start with an idea, a cause, a heartfelt need to deliver a timely word for the moment. I like to start with the cover. Recently, I was sitting at my desk doing academic research, and I came upon the picture of a gorilla. I sent my editor an email and said, "I have found the cover for my next book." For years I believed the wicked lie that, "You can't tell a book by its cover." Very false. I will now explain the reasons why the whole world should tell a book by its cover. Consider houses. Would a mansion have an interior that was decorated in Contemporary Shack Noveau? Or would there be a magnificent interior with a shack exterior? Not likely. Let me offer another example to prove my newly named Theory of Interior/Exterior Compatibility. Would you wrap a diamond ring in a paper bag? Next, consider the bruised banana. What do you expect to find inside?

Once I have my cover, I begin the writing process. The ape, oops, I mean the gorilla book will have a Daily Devotional format. A Daily Devotional format has the text perfectly divided into 365 Daily readings. A word to the wise, please do not wait for January to begin reading. No, no, no. You can start reading on any calendar date. I bought my first Daily Devotional in May and waited eight months to start. You may begin reading *Gorilla Lies* on any given day of the year. Ah yes, the title, *Gorilla Lies*. Another Different Strokes for Different Folks approach to writing. My advice is to begin with a catchy title and then write the text. Understanding the need for an irrefutable justification for this approach, I offer an academic reference. I humbly justify my writing style and declare that it is not backwards, instead it is forward thinking. If you are unsure if 'forward-thinking' applies, here is one dictionary's application of the term. "Forward-thinking companies use a combination of order to invoice quality and collections automation technologies to arrest the growing source of profit erosion." I agree.

Oops

We all have our 'Oops' moments. Spill? Oops. Drop? Oops. Typically, 'Oops' is used for spills and drops. But what if you crash into someone's car, fence, or front door? Oops. Overdrawn at the bank? Oops. Lost the job? Oops. Stock Market mistake? Oops, oops, oops. Used traditionally for coffee spills and broken dishes, I am recommending that 'Oops' be elevated to include more significant moments. Why? It's simple. If we use 'oops' for big mistakes, it lessens the pain. Your child goes to jail. Oops. Missed the flight? Oops. Instead of guilt by association, this is 'trivial by association.'

If we use 'oops' for big mistakes, it lessens the pain.

I hear you asking if I have ever considered counseling. Yes, I've considered counseling. Not for me. I've considered it as a career choice. Strange question. I am the first to admit that I lack the patience to be a counselor. My response to someone who returns session after session with the same issues would be, "Didn't we discuss this *last* week? Look, I told you what to do about your mother-in-law, your alcoholic husband, your tendency to steal. Don't you have anything new that is wrong?" So, thank you for associating me with counseling; I may have the wisdom but not the patience. Saying, "Don't worry about it" lacks the expected professional edge.

I did counsel a friend who was having major marital issues, I told her to seek professional help. The couple made an appointment with their religious cleric. He told them to, "Go home and stop fighting." Oops.

And the Winning Name Is . . .

I love it when names have meaning. For example, the last name of Miser. Makes you think, doesn't it? The name Patricia means snob. That's a fit. What about names like Little or Moron? Just kidding, no one has the last name of Moron. I know a financial adviser who changed his name to 'Cashmore' which opens up the possibility of a large group to be named Moron. It worked for him, and well, maybe Moron is a real last name. Here are some names that might bring a smile: Annette Curtain, Anne Teak, Aretha Holly, Barry Cade and I will end this list with Bob Apple.

But . . . but I can't stop thinking about the dentist I went to whose name was Royal Fink III. Why did his parents, his grandparents and his great grandparents do that to their baby boys? According to Webster's dictionary a 'fink' is a person who is strongly disliked. Not a good start but why couple that with the first name of 'Royal' and then carry on the tradition for three generations? It reminds me of a Woody Allen story. Woody's uncle leaned over the railing in a movie theater balcony and fell on his head. He went back and did this every day for a week so that no one would think that his initial fall was a mistake.

Not to be anti-religious and especially toward my own group of believers but I have always been confused with the first name of 'Oral.' I have never dared to ask anyone, "What kind of a name is that?" Maybe it's one of those southern things that we Yankees pride ourselves on not understanding. In the 1970's I met a woman who named her son Sidhartha. Years later, I heard that she became a born-again Christian. I guess she shortened his name to Sid.

A name is something we carry for life, use every day but have no input. It is a decision our parents make that has a long and lasting effect. This is very unfair. My middle name is a total embarrassment. My parents decided to combine the first names of two aunts: Aunt Betty and Aunt Josie. Voila—Betty Jo. The name Betty Jo puts me in a different geographic region from New York. Being both a Patricia and a Betty Jo is at best contradictory and confusing. STOP! WAIT! Could this be the reason I never get blonde jokes?

A name is something we carry for life, use every day but have no input.

Please, Honk and Thank You

This election year, I put a political bumper sticker on my car. I will not create confusion by revealing which party had my support but having a political bumper sticker was a first for me. I like reading bumper stickers, but I have never put one on my car. Because my car does not have a bumper, I placed two political bumper stickers a few inches apart on the back of my hatchback. I thought they looked pretty darn good. I decided to do an online search into the world of bumper stickers. Bumper sticker authorities claim that bumper stickers enable people to communicate and express themselves. I also read that they are difficult to remove. Bummer. Bumper stickers are becoming passe and being replaced by social media. Well, as usual I am decades behind since I am only starting my bumper sticker communication and self-expression journey. Now I aggressively seek out and read people's bumper stickers to meet people, make friends and drive dangerously.

Oooh, here's an interesting one—I will comment and connect, "Hello, I see that you are a vegetarian, have a chihuahua, and practice yoga"—but you just turned at the stop sign and "Come back. I'm a vegetarian and I have two cats. Wait. Stop. Let's talk . . . I didn't really vote for . . . ."

Is This News Fit to Print?

This may sound extreme, but I urge you to stop reading The News. Do not read, listen to, or watch any national or international news for a week. If you live in Florida, you will want to stay connected to the local report just in case there is a sink hole on the next block or the alligators have organized and are headed for town; but other than that, take a break from the worries of the world.

There was an article in this morning's paper. STOLEN PARROT RETURNED BUT TRAUMATIZED. Who can awaken to headlines like that and not shudder? The victim was taken from a pet shop and was later found. The incident was a labeled a 'drug related crime' leaving readers unsure if that meant that the thief was acting under the influence of drugs or intended to sell the parrot to buy drugs. Please clarify, the world needs to know.

It has been suggested that reading the paper gives people a sense that their life is good compared with the news. This is true. I read about a man who was knocked from his fishing boat by a sea lion. The sea lion dragged him under the water. I don't do potentially dangerous things like fishing and my problems certainly do not reach that magnitude.

A very sick crime occurred in rural Florida several years ago. A local radio news reported that a pregnant goat had been stolen and replaced with a nonpregnant goat. I love living in North Florida, but I also read that a local church group believes that cats can be demon possessed and they were linked to the death of area household pets. This does warrant reporting. If someone thinks my little kitty Sabrina is an agent of Satan, I want to know. Because I am a 'Believer' this is very confusing. I will take a deep breath, wait a minute and assume that they are correct. I am not necessarily convinced that pets can be demon possessed but let's accept that neighborhood cats have been demonized. Is killing them the answer? What ever happened to the power of prayer? There are dark forces at work on planet earth, but would I kill a demon possessed cat? No more than I would steal a parrot or replace a pregnant goat with a non-pregnant goat.

Another favorite news article from my cache of news trivia involved a crime worth bringing to public attention. There is someone who holds the slob bar so high that the average mess pot cannot compete. A recent news article described an apartment that was condemned by the Health Dept. because there were hundreds of rats which could have been eliminated if the resident had taken out the trash. They had not done this for over ten years. Who likes to take out the trash? I do it. I don't like to do it but something deep inside tells me that the consequences are not worth the risk. My ideal garbage solution is condo living where you put the trash down a shoot next to the elevator.

A friend from Maine shared a copy of her town paper with me. I enjoyed reading about a hardy elderly woman who found a dead chicken frozen under her house. She brought it inside, put it in the microwave and then gave it CPR. The chicken lived. When I excitedly shared that story at a CPR training class, the response was a long awkward silence.

To eliminate news trauma, I stay informed with moderation and have replaced watching the news with food shows. I enjoy Guy's Grocery Games, Chopped, and Beat Bobby Flay. If there is a food crisis, I will be ready.

Yummy Catfish

Catfish is an interesting word. It is sad that a fish looks like its nemesis the cat. Very odd and very meaningless. Odd? Meaningless? The essential criteria I use when I write. Catfish have long catlike whiskers and walk on the ground. Do I really want to eat these? I mean, "Oh yes, fried catfish. Yum." Cats eat fish; and this innocent animal has the physical characteristics of the species that wants to have it for dinner. Does this contradictory naming of God's creatures apply to other animals? Looking at other animal names that are joined together, such as 'horsefly,' and 'bulldog,' none of these carry the impact of catfish. Even 'birddog' doesn't match the catfish combo. Speaking on behalf of all animals who were cruelly given the name of their killer due to a biological mishap in which they played no part and using my courtroom 'legalese' I ask you, "Is this justice?

Forced to live in the mud, catfish make a drumming sound when distressed. Did I hear someone say, "Boring"? Oh. Boring? Just how boring is it that a 646-pound catfish was caught in Thailand in 2005? I have always envied people who are recognized as authorities in a particular area. That's it! The perfect place for me to be an expert is catfish. No competition. Who would question my claims? Miss Pat—Catfish

Speaking on behalf of all animals who were cruelly given the name of their killer due to a biological mishap in which they played no part and using my courtroom 'legalese' I ask you, "Is this justice?

Expert. "As I was saying, there was a 646-pound catfish caught in Thailand, but these occurrences are rare. The humble but impressive catfish is a global creature found on every continent except Antarctica." Could this make me rich? Now that I have reached 'seniorhood' is this the niche I have been searching for all these years? I have skimmed the surface of subjects from traditional Aztec Art to intergalactic molecular disturbances and all along it was 'catfish' waiting to be the focus of my intellectual pursuit. But wait a minute, do I really want my focus to be directed toward something that is served in the South with hush puppies? 'Hushpuppy,' now there's an interesting word.

TASTY VERY TASTY

Raising the Coffee Bar

There is nothing like an early morning bike ride to a local luncheonette for a cup of coffee 'straight-up.' Before the advent of specialty coffee shops (yes, there was a time when we did not have them) luncheonettes had a counter that was referred to as the coffee bar. If you are unsure of the word 'luncheonette,' you probably understand the word 'bar.' Coffee was not an acceptable drink in our house, so by necessity, I began my day with an early morning bike ride along the beach, no traffic, fresh air, the cruel consequence of being a part of the 1970's health food movement. In our healthy house, coffee was the forbidden drink so I was forced to indulge at the local luncheonette.

Coffee is more than just a drink. The female tradition of the coffee klatch goes back to my mother and grandmother. My mother used to drink her coffee black, a somewhat manly choice. Mom was unique and so were her coffee drinking habits. She would order coffee by the half cup. If a confused waitress brought her a full cup, mom would pour half into her water glass and continually ask for half cup refills. This assured her that she would always be drinking it hot. Temperature is important. In keeping with this family tradition, I ask for a few ice cubes when ordering my coffee to cool it down. It is sort of like the three bears—not too hot, not too cold, but just right.

I will now suggest that the entire world, not just Americans, would be unable to give up drinking coffee. Why? Consider the social bonding effect and the potential unification of diverse people groups. We all want coffee, and we want it first thing in the morning. Universality. It's the Brotherhood of Bean. A bond that unites us. "Stop, don't shoot. Do you drink coffee? I drink coffee too." We are all one. Coffee unifies but it is also age specific. Children don't get coffee. It is an 'Adults Only' drink providing instant age superiority.

We all want coffee, and we want it first thing in the morning.

Next, let's consider the Boston Tea Party. Tea, the colonial beverage of choice, was dumped into the water. If the prerevolutionary addiction to tea matched our current addiction to coffee, I submit that we would be bowing to the queen. Would you be willing to give up coffee? All the coffee gets dumped into the water. NO TAXATION WITHOUT REPRESENTATION, but no coffee? In keeping with this patriotic theme, I humbly offer my variation of Paul Revere's Ride:

Listen my children and do not fear
The midnight ride of Paul Revere.
On the 18th of April in '75
Before the coffee did arrive
The patriots dumped into the sea . . .
The oh so boring British Tea.

If I have offended tea drinkers, I apologize. I try not to offend people, especially my readers. Let me soothe hurt feelings by recommending either the Grande Mocha Caramel Tea, or the Double Pumpkin Spice with whipped cream.

Thank You, Johnny Appleseed

It's September and on the weekend, I went apple picking. After eating way too many bowls of homemade applesauce, I have decided to advocate nominating the all-American apple to be our National Fruit. You may find yourself asking, "Do we have a National Fruit?" Washington has fruitcake, but fruit? The answer is "Yes." The eagle, bald and somewhat frightening, shares National prestige with a chosen fruit. That chosen fruit is none other than . . . the blueberry. What! Don't get me wrong, I like blueberries. I just think that apples are more deserving of the National Fruit title. I want my National Fruit to be crisp. I want it to dangle majestically from a tree, and not be a small berry plucked from a bush. If we look beyond these physical characteristics to the history of apples, they easily trump the lowly blueberry.

Superior to mere muffin or pancake fame, apples have achieved notoriety in the key areas of religion, education and health. Consider the apple's history, going back to the Garden of Eden. What other fruit could have caused the downfall of man? A banana? A grape? No, only the apple could have tempted Eve to lose it all for one simple bite. It was then and there that apples got linked to The Tree of Knowledge and fast forward a few thousand years, and we have the bring the teacher an apple tradition. Today, you can't bring your teacher an apple because all food products brought to schools have to be commercially prepared, labeled and wrapped but none the less, the apple theme can still be found decorating America's classrooms. If history were not enough, apples come with a medical endorsement: An Apple a Day Keeps the Doctor Away. (Away, how far away? Does this work for the dentist and the dermatologist?) Even the cliché, "As American as Apple Pie" should give apples the honor of being our National Fruit. Have you ever heard "As American as a blueberry muffin?" No. Never.

Have you ever heard "As American as a blueberry muffin?"

I would be remiss if I didn't consider the competition. What other fruit could upset the grocery cart and claim the title of National Fruit? Hawaii might nominate the pineapple, but it would be competing with Wisconsin's cranberries and the Florida orange. If we move forward with a Johnny Appleseed logo, I predict that apples will win. A focused campaign targeting Wisconsin, Hawaii and Florida, will enable us to take those states and replace blueberries in the next National Fruit election. "Miss Pat, there is no next National Fruit election. The blueberries have it. They've already won."

Cupcake Wars

I enjoy baking. Baking is the perfect hobby. Low cost and safe it meets my fuss budget criteria. Unlike a cousin who long ago wowed me by whipping up a cake while texting and feeding twins, I prefer a more laid-back approach. Surprised? Before baking, everything else must be done and I mean *everything*. Baking requires the perfect environment. A clean house, the right lighting, music, no distractions . . . basically between midnight and three a.m. Inspired by the baking competitions that I enjoy watching on TV, last week I made cookies that gave a whole new meaning to the words dry and tasteless.

Baking requires the perfect environment.

The cookie competitions are impressive, but the cake competitions are over the top. Putting marble to shame, professional cake artists create life size cakes in the shape of people, animals and even furniture. Defying gravity is not enough, these cake structures must also pass the taste test. I don't know how they do it. I watched as one team created a Christmas cake in the shape of a reindeer with a life size Mrs. Claus happily feeding hot chocolate to a cluster of cake elves. The holiday baking shows are a seasonal treat, but my favorite

TV baking competition can be enjoyed year-round. It is an understatement to say that I am captivated by Cupcake Wars. I do more than watch, I am glued to the set. I even enjoy watching repeat shows. I know who will win, but I hang on every delicious moment with a level of attention unmatched in my academic life. Such drama, such emotion, such frosting, I love it.

The cupcake culture is a 21st Century phenomena, but I made my share of cookies, brownies, and cakes. Where was Cupcake Wars when I could have joined the fray? I had no idea that the humble art of flour, sugar, eggs, and frosting could hold such drama. "Your butter cream, it is tasteless, but I love your bourbon filling." I watch as a grown woman emotionally flips from utter dejection to joy. The contestants are not home cooks; they are the owners of bakeries or head bakers, and they are there to win. "This is war. I am here to win," declares Tiffany, who is wearing a little pink skirt with a matching pink bow in her hair. Not the lawyer crowd, the women on Cupcake Wars have their own style and it is more Barbie than Ken. No black pants suits on this show.

My ability to sit and watch for hours surprises me, but I draw a parallel to men who sit, and watch sports all day. I am knitting so I can put a check in the being productive box. Recently, I sent my daughter a text, "Watching Cupcake Wars, it's a mother / daughter team, we can do this!" The fact that she doesn't bake is not considered. Undaunted by reality,

I continue, "I know the two of us can meet the challenge to create three cupcakes that capture the essence of competitive bull riding." Bull riding? I like a challenge but a bull riding cupcake? YES! I've got this. How about a bourbon filled dark chocolate cupcake with baked meringue that is covered with finely chopped nuts to represent saw dust? This is war and I'm here to win.

Cornbread Angel

A recent addition to our Thanksgiving table is homemade cornbread. No, I am not from the South but I lived in Florida long enough to warmly welcome grits and cornbread into my culinary world. Last week, I volunteered to prepare cornbread muffins to bring to a women's book club event. Retirement and volunteering go hand in hand. Unfortunately, the scenario went like this.

Batch #1 Homemade, from scratch of course, this is Miss Pat you're talking to, and well, quite frankly, they tasted like the main ingredient was sand.

Batch #2 Careful, careful, measure carefully, level cups, no mishaps, and—Voila. Batch #2 tasted like my pillow.

I love our free market economy, but it can be challenging in a baking crisis. I didn't have two or three or four product choices, I had four hundred choices. Use a Mix. Don't use a Mix. Cornmeal, Cornbread, Cornbread Mix, I stood for a long time in the baking section of a chain supermarket. Read carefully, don't be hasty, don't buy the wrong product. I am looking for Cornmeal not Mix, for Cornbread, yes muffins, and now it is a choice of white or yellow. Do I want white cornmeal or yellow cornmeal? At this point I didn't want either. We'll have Chili with blueberry muffins. They'll love it.

I know from Batch #1 that I want fine, not coarse cornmeal. This is confusing. Which store had the Gluten Free? Oh, I almost forgot, the key words that I must find are Gluten Free. So, to summarize, I was looking for Gluten Free, fine, white or yellow cornmeal. Should I get the mix? I was told not to use a mix, but the mix was Gluten Free and reading the label, it only required milk not buttermilk and no butter. The pound of butter will come later while eating, to slip the dry sucker down.

Why are there so many choices? One chain supermarket cannot be counted on to carry the same products when it comes to cornbread, cornmeal, mix, muffin stuff. Which store had the mix? Where did I see the mix that required milk only? I went to four of the stores in one chain, and then two in another, and then to the wholesale market and then to the boutique market. Why should I be confused? Am I starting to hate the South? I'm from New York. Why am I doing this? And then, then . . . an Angel.

An Angel appears and says, "Oh. No problem. You want to use this White Cornbread Mix". She holds up a package. "I do?" "Yes," says the Cornbread Angel. "Where did you get that? I have been to every market in town and sorry Angel, you are wrong, I know I saw *that* brand, but it wasn't cornbread mix it was . . . everything else. How do they do it? How do they make Muesli, Oatmeal, Soy Flour, Wheat Flour, Cereal? How, how?" I collapse sobbing. "There, there," says the Cornbread Angel. "They do make it all. They make it at their special Mill. Now, dry your tears, get up and go to this store. You can get it here." She scribbles a name on a note pad. "Did you go to this store? Here's their number. Call them." How did she do that? Well, blankety blank blank. I didn't go there; I went everywhere else. "Oh, thank you Cornbread Angel." Faster than a rising muffin, I raced to the recommended grocery. "It's here! It's here! The right product, the one that will keep me from failure and shame." I grabbed six bags. Lordy, these are expensive, a whole bag makes only twelve muffins. Who cares?

And so, Miss Pat wowed them with her cornbread muffins made from a mix, Gluten Free, milk only, not buttermilk. She served them with honey. Y'All enjoy.

A Piece of Cake

I love cake. Cake is not only delicious; it is art. When it comes to cake art, I am very conservative. I do not like the current trend to shape cakes into everything from a puppy to a motor-cycle. "No, no, no." says Miss Pat, the cake art connoisseur. I do not want to see a cake shaped like a mermaid or a swan; I want to see a cake that looks like a cake but one that is beautifully decorated. I do allow for cakes to be shaped like gift boxes but that is where I draw the line.

My love of cake and my use of cake to solve everything, can be traced back to my favorite childhood book, *The Story of Babar*. Babar, a young elephant, is orphaned then rescued by a kind old lady who takes him first to buy new clothes and then to a patisserie.

Wanting the best for my children, I remembered Babar and introduced them to what I call Cake Culture. School days began with an early morning bakery stop. After school, we went to the local French bakery for a chocolate croissant. Now that we are all fat, have rotted teeth, and great memories, maybe I need to rethink Babar. I know he made it back to the jungle and married

School days began with an early morning bakery stop.

his childhood love Celeste, but did he stop wearing clothes and going to the pastry shop? What about his fancy red sports car? Shouldn't I have loved a different story? Where are my values? Let me think . . . I liked Cinderella, but she grew up to marry a prince and lived in a castle. There was really no book that I liked more than *The Story of Babar*. I like a good plot. First shopping, then the pastry shop, you live with a kind old lady and then return to the homeland and are crowned Ruler of All.

Babar was written by a Frenchmen and what I love about French culture is that they know the importance of the Patisserie. Cake gets its own bakery, which is not to be confused with the Boulangerie where bread is sold. Who would be so foolish as to mix bread and cake in the same shop? Alas, alack, poor bread. Once the staff of life, it is now a scorned morsel unfit for human consumption. The revered staff of life, the humble, it will keep me alive if there is nothing else, *bread*, is out. Who would have believed that such a thing could happen?

If you haven't guessed, I take food very seriously. Putting my cake compulsion aside, I raised my children to eat healthy food. No additives. No preservatives. Everything fresh and made from scratch. When my daughter was in college, she revealed a horrible truth. I had to say something. The conversation went something like this, we were at a gas station:

Jessica: I'll have a beef jerky. (to the clerk)
Mom: Jessica, Jessica, I can't believe what just happened. It can't be true.
Jessica: Sorry, Mom. It started in Art School.
Mom: Jessica, it goes against everything you've been taught, our whole way of life.
Jessica: I like it, it's chewy.
Mom: I said nothing about the boyfriend, then not graduating, but this . . . I need to sit.

I guess other parents have had the dreaded *it was all for nothing* moment. I don't know, you try to raise them right but then one day they are eating beef jerky and pork rinds. I threw that in for effect; she's never eaten pork rinds. At least I think she has never eaten pork rinds.

Guilty as Charged

Why do I think that coffee is not supposed to be bitter? So bitter that I take one sip and want to spit it out. I will not alienate any readers by discussing individual brands of coffee because bitter seems to be everywhere. Large commercial brands and small-town breweries all serve the bitter brew. Sometimes the coffee is so bitter that I compare it with drinking hot tar. Not that I have ever started my day with a cup of hot tar, but my point is made.

How do I know that bitter is not how good coffee should taste? I compare it with the cup I get at my favorite French bakery. Not bitter, it is smooth and delightfully yummy. If this is true, why am I drinking bitter coffee instead of enjoying myself at the French bakery? The Realtor in me will rise up and answer. Location. Location. Location. My favorite bookstore sells bitter coffee. I go there because the atmosphere is desirable. I am surrounded by readers and by people who like to hang out in bookstores. The bookstore has skyrocketed their appeal by adding . . . drum roll please . . . delicious cakes. Need I say more?

The two indulgences that satisfy my life-long need to experience guilt are a convenient one stop shop. Guilt is not just a product of caffeinating myself and devouring sweets. I have been charged with a literary crime that needs to be addressed. I have been told (by me) that my writing is too personal and immature. I agree with myself concerning these unflattering adjectives. Maturity has never been one of my life goals, and if I am not mature by now, it isn't going to happen. As for the second negative description 'too personal', I can only say "Of course." Everyone knows that immature people are self-centered. Maturity is outward focused, immaturity is not. My writing is all about me, the big M. My experiences, my ideas, my thoughts. Do I have a defense? Yes. Bitter coffee made me do it.

> *Guilt is not just a product of caffeinating myself and devouring sweets.*

Le Petit Dejeuner

I love holiday food. Is there anything better than turkey, gravy, mashed potatoes, stuffing, rolls and yum, yum, yum? Maybe I just like food. Let's face it, food is something that we all enjoy. Food unifies and bonds us together. So far no one has found a way to live and not eat.

I love to visit my daughter because she expects me to cook. "Good Morning. Rise and shine, it's time for French toast," I cheerily sing out to the two not morning people who lack my enthusiasm for everything. The two 'don't talk to me before noon' sleepers are my daughter and granddaughter. Grammy has come to set the world back on happy, like it or not.

I traveled to Arizona to help my daughter during a difficult semester in grad school. I came for three months and stayed three years. Just a thoughtful heads up to anyone who may have considered inviting me for a visit. Not to be too invasive, after three months I moved to my own apartment across a courtyard from 'the girls.' A healthy distance apart, we were still able to share pots, pans and pounds. I make the best French toast, my daughter makes the best bacon, (she bakes it) and we gained about fifteen pounds each.

Who wouldn't be able to make the best French toast after watching marathon episodes of Chopped and Beat Bobby Flay? I love, love, love cooking shows. "And for your final challenge you will make a dessert using eel, peanut butter, and coconut." Then they do it. It is so amazing. In one show the challenge was to only use meat and a contestant made pork ice cream for dessert! I don't just watch, I cheer. "Go Bobby!" It must be very annoying to the family members who are happy to have me glued to the sofa. I have noticed that a lot of the contestants, when asked why they entered the competition, respond by saying that they want to make their children proud. Huh? The old fashioned me will now take over and say, isn't that in reverse? I thought kids were supposed to make their parents proud. A contestant has to win Chopped before their children will look up to them? Quite possibly I am the only viewer with this negative analytical response, but it also seems too hard to do. What if you don't win? Of course, this is coming from a woman who has already won The Best French Toast award.

Cooking in Arizona came to an end. One day it happened. I had to get out. I was trapped in a foreign land. I started telling myself (and anyone else who would listen) that if I ever make it back to Florida, I will never go west of the Mississippi again. I wanted to see green foliage, feel humidity, smack mosquitoes. I missed a Florida backyard with lush green trees and lizards flapping their orange throat flappers. Give me Florida or give me death.

" But Miss Pat, what about French Toast and happy mornings stuffing your face with bacon?" This Grammy still loves to visit, and when I do, it's "Rise and shine, time for French Toast."

So Real

I am creating a new breakfast cereal. It has been said that how you start your day is important. Breakfasts are important. They set the tone and the energy level for the day. With that in mind it is time to rescue breakfast from the world of dry cereal, and pop tarts. I plan to create a breakfast cereal that will start each day with a blast and will keep the energy going well past three, four and five p.m. My product will be nutritious, wholesome and I refuse to acquiesce to circles, squares, or flakes. Should I go with mush? No. I love oatmeal but let's be honest, oatmeal lacks the desired 'blast' element. I have it! Mini omelets that come to life when milk is added. Voila! I can work on the recipe later. The important marketing plan comes first.

A successful blast into your day cereal needs a name that will propel it from the shelf to your grocery cart and that name is . . . drum roll please, . . . or better yet, spoons tapping cereal bowls . . . the name will be SUNRISE SURPRISE. No. That sounds like a cheap motel. The name will be . . . SO REAL. Each box of SO REAL will be packed with a special treat. Each box will have a teeny, tiny book to read while eating the cereal. This is a part of my anti-electronic diversion plan. Too many breakfasts are spent staring at cell phones, and scrolling emails for that all important message. The teeny tiny book will have READ ME on the cover inspired by the classic *Alice in Wonderland* and inside there will be a motivational verse or a thought for the day. "Nice, Miss Pat. Will the thought for the day be a quote from a famous historian or philosopher? A Bible verse?" Well, not exactly, I was thinking of something a little more contemporary. "Oh? I thought you were very conservative, what are you thinking?" True, but I am open to certain secular ideas that enhance and promote a high level of spiritual reality provided they are not day to day trash. "Such as?" Maybe, Don't Worry Be Happy or Alfred E. Newman's classic What Me Worry? "I don't know Miss Pat, mini-omelets, Bob Marley, Mad Magazine. Why not do something with chocolate? Chocolate is always a winner."

Roses Are Red

Fame has a price. My readers are starting to ask some very personal questions. Last week someone asked me, what tea do I drink. A response is necessary to avoid any false rumors. Are you sitting down? In addition to coffee, I do drink tea. Because I have a 'no product endorsement' policy, I will discreetly refer to the tea I drink as The Rose. If you aren't familiar with The Rose and still have a grandparent living, this is probably the tea that they drink. Not wanting to conform to the media hype for cool; I walk away from the brands that have flooded the market in the past twenty years. Thirty years? Time flies. The Rose is not gluten free. It is not organic. It is not environmentally friendly but, but . . . .it comes with a little ceramic animal in every box. Can you believe it! Each box is packed with a little friend to sit next to my cup while it brews. The Rose has always provided this emotional support. Does it get any cuter than this? And the price is so right, 100 bags for under $5.00 *plus* a little walrus! Way to go!

Please note, the little animals are not plastic. When I was a girl, I collected small porcelain animals. This is the electronic age, and The Rose is still packaging a miniature duck, horse, or whatever into every box. Amazing. I asked a friend from England which tea she drinks and if she had switched to an

American brand. You guessed it; she said that she likes The Rose because it is the most like British tea.

Selecting your tea culture is important. Do you want to drink British style, or Asian? Do you want herbal? Something similar to an identity crisis is the tea culture affiliation. If you go British, as I have done, then you drink your tea with milk and sugar. If you choose the Asia side of the equation, you are not using milk or sugar but possibly a squeeze of lemon. This is important. A mature adult needs to know where to cast their tea drinking ballot in order to reap the benefits of their brew. And just how do you brew your tea? Do you use a tea pot? The Rose is plebeian enough to be in bags. It is not a loose tea product, but some folks brew their tea bags in a fine china tea pot. Hmm . . . I know someone who does that.

Globalization has changed everything, and my guess is that countries that were founded on a bedrock of tea are probably now a part of the 'Coffee Culture.' That's okay; beans, leaves, twigs, whatever it is that you brew—identity marketing has you covered. The big incentive for my choice of tea is the gift packed into each box. What other food products are willing to do this? Uh-oh, I am starting to think. What other food products *should* be doing this and what would be their free gifts? Unable to resist an opportunity to explore something meaningless, I accept the challenge. Here is a list of products paired with their potential gifts.

> *Unable to resist an opportunity to explore something meaningless, I accept the challenge.*

1. Whole Wheat bread—little wagons carrying shafts of wheat in from the field.

2. Almond Milk—a mini cow.

3. Sticky Candy like the one that pulled the caps off two of my teeth . . . a wind-up dentist.

4. Fakin' Bacon—three wind up pigs that roll on the table, point at you and laugh.

5. All brands of designer coffee—a piece of gold jewelry.

So, put the kettle on, line up your porcelain animal friends—it's time to relax with a cup of tea.

Still Talking Turkey

Thanksgiving is one of my favorite holidays. This year I am visiting my daughter in Texas. I arrived a day early and in time to help with the grocery shopping. Shopping for groceries is a part of the fun. Yes, I said fun. There is something about pushing a cart and strolling the aisles. I may have an empty closet, but I will never have an empty refrigerator. When the shopping is done, we are ready for tomorrow's big day.

My favorite part of preparing a turkey dinner is to fry up the liver and eat it while the turkey roasts. Turkey liver is delicious. Did I hear someone say, "Yuck"? Alas, alack, I found the neck but . . . but where is the bag with the giblets? (giblets is the polite word for liver, heart and other rejected body parts.) My hand goes in; my hand comes out. No giblet bag. Other side. My hand goes in; my hand comes out. Ditto, the same. Okay folks, what's going on here? I want my turkey liver and I want it now. Even more embarrassing would be to roast the turkey with the liver still in the bag tucked way inside the bird. (Not something that has ever happened to me.)

Two independent turkey inspectors are called to the scene and the verdict is the same. No giblet bag. Maybe because it is a Kosher turkey? Okay maybe, I am not sure why, but okay it is agreed that there is no (sob) liver for this grandma to cook and enjoy. Life has its disappointments. I will move forward.

Next, we brine the turkey. Brine? If my son is reading this, he will smile. He is the first in our family to discover the now essential brining step. Being novices to the brine process, my daughter purchases a Brine Kit which includes a large plastic bag, a packet of brining powder, a packet of seasoning for after the brine and best of all, DIRECTIONS. We find a bucket and start the brine. The bag goes in the bucket (dear Liza, dear Liza) then we add two gallons of liquid, the powder and oops let's not forget the turkey. This all goes into the frig overnight and it is extraordinarily heavy. Are you taking notes? Well, don't. We left it in the brine too long, but no one will notice. Thanksgiving Day, El Tomador is loving rubbed spa style with soft butter, then the herb packet and voila—into the oven. After an extended debate about what is 15 x 15 divided by 60, we reach an agreed upon cooking time. Unfortunately, Tom must share his oven space with baked mac & cheese. Hours later, we are still unsure of how many (15 pounds @ 15 minutes a pound?) it is Turkey Time and grandma loves to make the gravy. Daughter makes the mashed potatoes. Happy Thanksgiving. We are very, very grateful.

Life has its disappointments. I will move forward.

LIFE, LIBERTY, AND THE PURSUIT OF HAPPINESS

A Thrifty Addiction

I am addicted to thrift shop shopping. It's the thrill of the hunt. You don't know what you are looking for but there is a chance you might find it. Somewhere waiting for me under piles of junk is that one of a kind, wonderful, unexpected something that for only $2.00 can be mine.

I have a passion for baskets and thrift shops have the best baskets in town. I am not talking about discarded Easter baskets. Thrift shops have antique baskets, sewing baskets, baskets for books, baskets for toys, baskets, baskets and more baskets. Last week I stood in front of a display of baskets and thought, "I want them ALL." If I buy them all, I can resell them at flea markets! I will be a dealer of fine wicker, a collector, a basket connoisseur! It was more than I could stand. Since I was walking, I left with what my arms could carry. I now have a porch closet filled with wicker baskets. My adult children look worried when I display my wonderful wicker wares. "Obviously, mom is now nuts but maybe we can get her to join a book club."

The key to successful thrift shop shopping is to revisit the territory often.

The key to successful thrift shop shopping is to revisit the territory often. If you visit the thrift shops often, you will quickly learn which ones offer the best prices for particular items. There is one shop that sells crystal and fine china at dollar store prices. There are also boutique thrift shops but frankly honey it's not worth it, the church and charity shops have the best clothing bargains. It is difficult to explain, but once you pay $5 for a designer bag, or skirt or whatever (I have bought Oleg Cassini whatever) there is no going back. You will never buy retail again. If you have no pride and love a deal, you will not only wear Missy's clothes, you will be thrilled when you find them.

On Book TV, I heard a presentation by an author who wrote *The Obsessive Mind of the Collector*. When does a thrift shopper turn into an obsessive collector? For me it was a Saturday at about 3:00 p.m. It also happens when you stop buying for yourself and start thinking, "Who can I give this to?" I found myself rummaging through boxes of old dress patterns. Old dress patterns? I stopped sewing years ago. I don't have a sewing machine. The answer is obsession. I can justify obsession. It takes your mind off reality and totally embraces you. Anything that absorbs your total attention is relaxing. You become lost in the moment.

And remember, this is a hunt and should be categorized with other hunting sports like fishing or animal hunting. Visualize shoppers going out before dawn in camouflage clothing, armed with shopping bags ready to bring home 'the big one.' Today, I could be bringing home the big one. Since I am walking, it can't be too big. When I return exhausted, take off my designer shoes, close my eyes under my natural feather quilt, and turn off my imitation Tiffany lamp; I smile. I have a closet full of wicker baskets.

Warm Fish

Everyone needs a cause, something to fight for—to believe in. Now that I am retired, I am an advocate for goldfish. Fish have been highly underrated as pets. When you finish reading this you will rethink the status of pet fish. Fish were the pets our parents hoped to get away with giving us. Consider the lone goldfish swimming in its bowl, so deserving of number one pet status. My life's goal is to make goldfish the Number One American Family Pet. One day, fish will earn the 'Man's Best Friend' title held way too long by dogs. Aquarium fish are not pets; they are aquarium fish. The practical advantages are obvious. No late-night walks, no poop scoop, no litter box.

Fish have been highly underrated as pets.

Let's go beyond the obvious and explore the fish/human connection. Our negative attitude toward fish is based on the 'cold fish' stigma. We casually declare that someone is a 'cold fish.' This is a wicked lie. I present to you the warm loving fish, a household pet of emotional quality equal to kitty or pup. Consider how rewarding it would be to be greeted by your excited fish jumping all over you making it impossible to navigate from the door to a table or counter to at least put down your purse, so you can offer fishy the lavish attention he so deserves. "Yes, yes, yes, I love you too, so happy to see you, oh I missed you so much, don't jump up, settle down. Does fishy want love? Off the furniture please." Or apply the kitty scenario to your scaled darling, "Look at you—so pristine sitting at the window. Does Momma's precious fishy want to sit on my lap?"

One of the deterrents to becoming the Number One Pet has been the inability to take your fish with you when you go out. Not anymore. Pet fish carriers will be available in colors that coordinate with cute fishy swimsuits. The carriers will have wheels, so you don't have to carry but can 'walk' you fish. Little fishy swimsuits will be produced by some entrepreneurial soul; puppy outfits having set a standard that fish-wear will surpass. Using the fish carriers, fish lovers will be able to take their finned friends with them when they travel.

Motels and restaurants will boast of being 'Scale Friendly.' Expect to see fish bumper stickers, I Love My Fish, or My Other Dog is a Fish. We will nostalgically consider 'Just a boy and his fish.' Doggy day care will be replaced with ponds for fish to socialize and play.

Now, let's be honest, a stumbling block to achieving Number One Pet status has been that we eat fish. We do not knowingly eat cat or dog. If we are to elevate goldfish to the status of man's best friend, we need to stop eating their cousins like tuna, salmon, and trout. Shellfish will always be okay.

Improved names are needed. I recommend names with character and importance like Jonah, or Leviathan. Once you have selected a name, purchased the products, the next is easy. Love your fish. We are told that love is a decision and not an emotion. After six or seven months of choosing to love your pet fish, you will notice a change in how people treat you, a change in how you view yourself. It's a life changing experience with a ripple effect. That said, it's time for me to take Mr. Bubbles for a walk.

M & M

I call this M & M because I have been asked to write about the men in my life and about living in Micanopy. Not one to ignore the possibility of a cute title, I have combined the two and Voila—M & M. Why would someone ask me to write about these two 'M' words? I was told that my writing is impersonal and that I need to share my life. Impersonal? I have written about the dentist, my adventures riding the city bus, even being scammed on the internet. So, it's personal you want, is it? Okay, I'll give you the nitty gritty personal. Sit back, close the door, turn off your phone and . . .

M #1. Write about the men in my life? Do you have a sticky note for me to use? Inquiring minds want to know if there is anyone significant? Well, for starters there's Bill. He comes around way too often and frankly he gets on my nerves. I have already written about Gym. I like him and if Bill hadn't interfered, I would have taken up with Gym a lot sooner. "Anyone else Miss Pat?" Let me think. Frank has always been in my life; and he can get me into trouble, but he's become more manageable since Les showed up. Les has been around too long. So long that he has left a Mark that only my guy friend Pat can smooth. Next and Justin time, Drew arrived to helped me with Art but Art was never a problem. I find Art very relaxing. And to close, I am happy to say that Dustin came into my life after Sandy and well that's pretty much it. Why?

M #2. Life has its embarrassing contradictions, weird juxtapositions, contradictory and contrasting occurrences. What am I talking about? I am talking about the Nudist Café and Scary Cat Fireworks. Rats! Why are they at the Interstate exit for the small historic town I call my retirement home? Micanopy was voted one of Huffington Post's Cutest Small Towns. We know from the highway billboards that at the Nudist Café they 'Bare All!' As for Scary Cat Fireworks, who knows? I guess they are dressed. I have changed the names to be politically correct and protect the guilty. Somehow these landmarks just don't fit with antique shops and a town that is one quaint block of one-hundred-year-old buildings.

> *Life has its embarrassing contradictions, weird juxtapositions, contradictory contrasting occurrences.*

When I have friends visiting and I need to direct them from the Interstate to Micanopy, it sounds like this: "You exit at the sign for the Nudist Café, yes, the one that says We Bare All. That's right. Good grief. Turn at the sign for Scary Cat Fireworks. No. No. Yes, it's open year-round. Follow the signs to Historic

Micanopy. Park in front of the ice cream parlor. Musicians will be playing on the porch. They are there every weekend. We have great bluegrass fiddlers. The building I live in is called Shady Oak; it's a former B & B that has been converted for long-term residents. Never mind about the Café, it's just for truckers coming off the highway; I promise you that it is not a part of the historic town. Yes, we wear clothes. *Historic,* not nudist. You'll love it. They filmed Doc Hollywood here; it is very quaint. Okay. Have a safe trip. What? Art, I'm involved with Art. No. Forget the café, I live above an ice cream parlor.

Probably Not

I am on a budget. Last week I treated myself to a bottle of Fish Oil Gummies. If you have taken fish oil in any other form, you will understand the motivation behind this splurge. The Fish Oil Gummies are sweet, chewy and have no after taste. Yum. Who knows what next month's special treat will be? I am eyeing a 50 lb. bag of pine kitty litter for my little darlings, but I don't want to go too wild.

I enjoy hearing that the economy is up but as usual I am out of step. I live in a wealthy town and when I go to the supermarket, I think about the possibility that the person standing next to me in line may be living in a three-million-dollar, two-bedroom condo. We are both buying groceries at the same store. Most of the cars in the parking lot are luxury vehicles and my fellow shoppers at least look to be very well off. Looking well off in a Florida resort town means that you are wearing designer exercise clothes. The dress is casual, but upscale casual.

I enjoy hearing that the economy is up but as usual I am out of step.

Do my fellow shoppers think that the raspberries are too expensive? What about walnuts? I casually glance into a cart looking for walnuts. No walnuts. I try not to be nosey but what else is there to do while waiting online? Read the magazine headlines? Buy gum or eye drops? I pick the magazine option and I am immediately confused. Somebody must buy these or else they would not be selling them but . . . who? Stand up. Admit it. Which one of my loyal readers has bought the magazine that will tell them why Prince Somebody was seen wandering the streets of London at two a.m. or how they can effortlessly lose thirty pounds eating sour cream dip and potato chips?

My favorite supermarket chain sells books, and they also sell Choice Books which are faith-based books. I have never bought a book at the grocery store. For that matter, I don't buy books, I use the library, but we have already established that I am out of step. Not that anyone else should choose the lowly library over a solid book purchase which being a writer; I can only promote as a legacy investment, similar to old clocks.

I am happy to announce that soon I will be selling a new book on Amazon so stay tuned, especially if you are under the age of five. My *Little Lion's Bedtime* has been reprinted and newly illustrated and after a wide distribution in Ethiopia and Germany it will be available in the U.S. for the first time in an all-English edition. I suggested that it be sold with a small stuffed lion cub wearing pajamas, but I was told to put that marketing scheme on hold.

I am advocating for creative pricing. If you live in a recently built downtown condo and long to read about a little lion who can't sleep, the price is a small percent of your annual gross income. If you come with sufficient proof that you live in a house that is under 500,000 you can get a discount. As for the little stuffed lion cub wearing pajamas, there will be choices, either plain cotton PJ's or 'designer' which will have the signature lion cub smiling on or above the pocket. In addition to selling *Little Lion's Bedtime* on Amazon, I will follow the example of Girl Scout Troop 203 and set up a table outside.

Successful Failure

My financial advisor suggested that I write a loser's handbook. Not easily offended, I accepted the challenge. I knew that I would have to do a lot of library research and that the project could take months, however the opportunity to collaborate with some of the world's finest losers was tempting. To begin, I prepared a questionnaire based on a random sampling of my life's experience. Although I consider myself to be a huge success, since I am not a snob, I will prepare guidelines for those less fortunate than myself. To begin, the term Born Loser is incorrect. Successful losing takes time, effort and planning. It is an acquired skill which can be perfected over a lifetime. This morning, I couldn't find anything, first it was my keys, then my wallet, then my car. I don't drive, so I must have also lost my mind.

Successful losing takes time, effort and planning. It is an acquired skill which can be perfected over a lifetime.

Today was the perfect day to begin writing *The Loser's Handbook: An Authoritative Guide to Successful Failure*. By noon, the book was finished, and I started a series of seminars; Lose Now—Ten Easy Steps,

Financial Freedom and Weight Loss, and How to Lose Your Perfect Soul Mate. Financial Freedom and Weight Loss is a revolutionary concept developed by a Swiss therapist. Years of research has shown that there is an undeniable connection between weight loss programs and a decline in finances. If you order now, a pre-publication opportunity, I will offer this series for only 4 payments of $79.99. (VHS) At no extra charge but for a love offering of $100 you will receive our newsletter, *I Can't Find Myself*. This dynamic resource provides maps, compasses and travel guides. We offer keys that find you and other items to help the common loser function in today's complex world.

Finally, I am excited to announce that there will be a Lose Cruise in May. Aboard replicas of the Nina, the Pinta, and the Santa Maria, we will combine the best of relaxation with intense lifechanging seminars. These seminars will be led by experts in the field, taking the lost to a level not yet experienced. With that said, my cat Fluffy and I are proud to present an excerpt from *Successful Failure*. These guidelines focus on all major areas of life: family, finance, career, and pets.

Choose to Lose

- Scatter yourself/diversify. This is the 'Jack of all trades but master of none' syndrome. I call it Life ADD. Do some painting, some writing, and a little sports. Spread this diversification out over a lifetime and you will find yourself (our goal) not far from where you started.

Develop low self-esteem. This is not hard your friends and family will help you.

Write everything down. This is a great waste of time. My handwriting is illegible, and my spelling is incorrect. If you have good handwriting and can spell, you would not be reading this.

- Misuse words. It's your language to isn't it?

- Never complete.

- Plan. Be a planner, then fail. That way no one can say that you didn't plan.

- Don't watch TV. I have never bothered to waste my time and pollute my thinking.

- Lead a healthy lifestyle. This is important if you are to blame yourself and not your crazy habits.

- Never use the spell chick.

I hope these suggestions have been helpful, and that you will consider joining us for the cruise.

May the Loss Be With You.

Mommy Get Your Gun

Are you worried about safety on New Year's Eve? People will be drinking, which implies that they will be more dangerous than usual. Well, you can put your worries aside because I have a new Safety-First plan that solves the problem. Not too long ago, I was surprised to learn that many women are now packing a concealed weapon. The pepper spray days are over and today women just aim straight and shoot. Of course, purse designers jumped to meet the demand and have produced stylish handbags with an extra compartment for mommy's pistol. I call it the Annie Oakley bag. One neighbor is hosting a series of gun licensing classes in her home. It is a 'women only' event with a waiting list for the next class. Tea and bullets?

Does my Safety-First plan include fire-arms training? No, I know better than to carry a gun. What if someone snatches my purse? I could get robbed and then shot. No, my safety plan is much simpler than that. I wear a whistle. I like it. It is on a long chain; and it reminds me of old movies I was too young watch. The police blew whistles and carried 'billy' clubs. I am not sure who Billy was, but I had an Aunt Josie who kept a billy club under her car seat and told me in a not very sugary tone that if anyone got in her car, she would use it. This is the same auntie who baked wonderful pies, so it took me awhile to process this aggressive aspect of her personality.

How did I come up with my new safety plan? Way back when, I had a purse siren which came in handy the day I tripped over a log on a deserted street and needed help. The problem with the siren is that in an assault you have to say, "Excuse me, I need to get the siren out of my purse." So, I have switched from a purse siren to a whistle. A whistle is easy access, and very, very loud. Do I plan to go to dangerous places? Not unless I am recreated into a totally different person.

When I was young, my parents frequently went to Times Square for their New Year's Eve big night out. One year, my dad's wallet was 'lifted.' Times Square is not on my New Year's Eve, good place to-be-list. I live in Sarasota, and a pineapple 'drops' at the special midnight moment. Hugs to Sarasota! But even with this creative spin on the celebration, I have trouble having fun on New Year's Eve because I don't understand the decision to have it be at this moment in time. Are we sure that this is the start of a new year? Counting from when? Moses? Adam? I need more facts. Too many other choices challenge the authenticity of the moment. There's the Jewish

New Year—you get a honey cake. Then there's the Chinese New Year, and people parade under a shared dragon costume. None of it resonates as true. Can I put truth aside, accept the consequences and know that when the pineapple drops it is maybe, possibly a New Year? Absolutely, as long as I have my whistle.

Say Goodnight, Gracie

At lunch last week, another teacher told me that her teenage son had 'In God We Trust' tattooed on his chest. She considered it to be an indicator of positive spirituality. I thought of my son's tattoos and said nothing. Have you noticed that businesses never have signs that say No Shirt—No Shoes—No Tattoos? I guess that such harsh discrimination would be illegal, but it would also bring financial ruin. I am in Arizona, and everyone has at least one tattoo. Everyone under the age of fifty. I am not under the age of fifty. I have no tattoos. My ears are pierced, just the lobes, one hole. I wear earrings. I have nothing on my tongue, nose, cheek, or lip. I like it that way.

My daughter asked if she should have her shoulder-to-shoulder tattoo colored. Perhaps it is too plain? I am past thinking, "Where did I go wrong?" and told her that "Sometimes less is more." More or less. Can I love someone with a tattoo? Yes, I can love people who have chosen to add ink to human flesh. Permanent ink. More permanent than permanent marker. Tattoos are *really* permanent. I know, there are ways to remove tattoos. This is done at a cost that is only available to people whose profession would inhibit them from getting tattoos in the first place.

Would I ever get a tattoo? Not only would I never get a tattoo, I will use this to take up the challenge to

Would I ever get a tattoo? write Ten Things I Would Never Do. Inspired by Ten Desserts You Should Never Serve to Your Guests, Ten Ways to Stay Happy and Still Pay Your Bills, Ten Lessons I Learned Driving My Kids to School, and Ten Things to Do in Less Than Ten Minutes, I proudly present Ten Things I Would Never Do. Can I be realistic and make it 100?

Here's the Top Ten:

1. Go on a Safari, a roller coaster, a Ferris wheel, a boat, a unicycle, a horse drawn wagon, a camel, all motorized or moving machinery that transports humans other than a car, a bus or a bike.

2. Eat sushi. This is one of the many things that sets me apart from contemporary society. I will never willingly eat sushi. I have to say this twice. I remain true to spinach dip and cheese balls for appropriate and desirable buffet items. When I look at sushi, I wonder, "What is that dark ring that looks like fish skin?" I am not anti-Asian.

3. I will never play a video game. Never have. Never will. I sound like Jed Clampet. It doesn't interest me at all.

4. I will never do a cartwheel. I would like to, but my remaining common sense says—impossible.

5. Surf naked. Self-explanatory.

6. Surf. Ditto

7. Dye my hair a pastel color. Blonde is not a pastel color.

8. Online dating. I might be lonely, but I am not crazy.

9. Pierce my tongue. No explanation needed. Doesn't that interfere with eating?

10. Burden myself with ten-item lists.

Does all of this reflect a chronic resistance to change? Change is everywhere. Today, the TV shows that I enjoyed growing up would not be tolerated. They would be pulled from the air for being racist, sexist and offensive. I agree, or at least I can acknowledge the criticism. For example, we watched Jack Benny ordering Rochester to get his hat and coat, Jackie Gleason making a fist and saying, "To the moon, Alice." And then there was George Burns with "Say goodnight, Gracie." What has this got to do with Ten Things I Would Never Do or tattoos? "Say good-night, Gracie."

Sole Analysis

I have decided that clothes don't make the man, shoes do, and as for "What's in your wallet?" "Who cares?" What I want to know is, "What's on your feet?" After years of study, I have reached some solid conclusions about women's shoes. Are you wearing Birkenstock? May I hold your shoe please. Hmmm let me see, solid leather, flat, arch support, okay, got it. You enjoy yoga, and eat organic, gluten free. Who's next? Do you wear Sneakers? Sandals? Flats? Heels that are so high that you need insurance to wear them? Bring on the shoes because I have a new hobby: Shoe Analysis. An online certification has provided the needed credibility to share my insights, which I affectionately refer to as sole searching.

What I want to know is, "What's on your feet?"

Analysis #1: WESTERN BOOTS

Boots provide a creative touch for the non-rancher. My daughter lives in Houston, downtown, away from cattle, horses, and manure. But it is a Texas downtown. She says wearing boots is an added perk to living in the Lone Star state. That's my girl! Decades ago, I happily wore cowboy boots here, there and everywhere. The fact that I lived in a beach resort didn't stop me from being cowgirl chic.

Analysis #2: EXCESSIVE SHOE BUYING

Not too long ago, I worked with a woman who bragged that she owned 100 pairs of shoes. I was tempted to whisper, "Honey, this is not something to brag about" but not one to rock the boat, I just smiled and said, "Wow." Let me see, what well known female dictator had that hobby? You are not wasteful or stupid you're MY BOSS! I love it! 100 pairs of shoes, how wonderful! Dorothy had special shoes. Do you have special red shoes that will take you out of Kansas? No? So sad. Keep buying and maybe one day you will get it right.

Analysis #3: SNEAKERS

Are you worried about slipping on a wet dock? Do you love to jog? Sneakers to the rescue. Sneakers were once reserved for special activities, but they are now a part of everyday footwear. Not in my Miss Prissy life, but it is true, most people wear sneakers most of the time. Why? They are comfy. Comfy? As in comfortable? I thought that's what slippers were for. Day to day footwear can be comfortable? Interesting. It's true, I am prejudiced against sneakers, flipflops, and excessive shoe buying.

I avoid conflict by staying off social media, but I have taken Sole Searching to the next level and offer online consultations. Using zoom, if you hold your shoe up to the camera, I will give a complete analysis. It is now time for a little introspection. Following the adage: 'If the shoe fits wear it,' I will analyze my own footwear choices. As mentioned, I have been known to wear cowgirl boots when I don't need them. I like Asian, embroidered, slipper style flats. Referring to my copious certification class notes, I will now hold a shoe, breathe deeply and concentrate. Think Miss Pat *think*, my footwear says . . . it says . . . I am a non-conformist, artistic, and indisputably nuts.

Late Bloomer—Baby Boomer

I am returning to college. I have advised my adult son that he can put SHE GRADUATED on my tombstone. When my peers are retiring, I will be entering the job market. I am learning that if you wait long enough school becomes fun. Last week I sat in a classroom for the first time in thirty years. I loved it. The procedure is so simple. You are given information, you learn the information, and then you are given a reward called 'a grade.' You pay money for this, a lot of money. I am pleased to scream from the roof tops that I am an A student. That had not been the case my first time around. I had always been a B student. It often bothered me, especially as an adult. Reflecting on my academic career, I saw it as a pattern for life. I was a B person. Definitely not C, D or F but regretfully not an A.

In my high school, the classes were given levels. I was in the second or B level classes. I was a B student in the B class. Was I a B homemaker and a B mother? I started to wonder what it would take to earn an A. More work? More time? Now I know. What it takes is an easier school and fewer classes. I have heard it said that nontraditional students may have acquired time management skills that traditional students lack. My best time management skill has been to take one class at a time. This is the secret strategy which brought my B up to an A. I need four more classes to earn an AA. This will take me two years. (I take summers off for maximum performance.) Once I have my AA, I will get a BA, then a MA and then a PhD. Unless I get a RIP. I could be

My best time management skill has been to take one class at a time.

teaching at a university when I am in my seventies! My mother lived to be ninety-four. This may be an answer to the problem of what to do with the elderly. Send us to school.

Another secret to my academic success is the undeniable parallel between age and the progressive decline in one's ability to have wild fun. This is very helpful. I have a definite advantage over the twenty-year-old sitting next to me with her head on her desk. Am I the only one in the room who is having a great time just being in class? I am older than the teacher and she is having an average time, a C time. Since I have returned to school, I grade everything. Shopping was a B experience. The TV show was a C. Our nation's industrial performance is slipping and needs more homework. My lunch was an A.

I am taking philosophy which gives me an excuse to contemplate the meaning of things. I have become very thoughtful and contemplative. I contemplate questions such as, "What if life is one big school, who is the principle? Am I in trouble? Am I late? Where's the nurse's office?" You may be asking, why didn't I finish my degree thirty years ago? An 'A' question. I went to school in Washington D.C. and spent more time taking the bus down Massachusetts Avenue, then going to class. In my sophomore year I discovered there was a sauna in the gym. Sauna, sauna, sauna. I earned an A in sauna. Then I started hanging out in the library and reading magazines, a sure sign of eminent failure. One day my parents came home, and I was in the family room watching TV. I had taken a plane, a limo, let myself in the house, made a sandwich and was not going back to school. I had WF (withdrew failing) from all but one class, Symbolic Logic. We did problems like:

> Patricia does not go to class.
> All students who pass go to class.
> Patricia will pass. T or F?

The correct answer is F and there were oooh so many of them.

The differences between college now and college then are many. There were no computers when I went to school. NO COMPUTERS. We had running water and there were cars. There were NO CELL PHONES. There were public phone booths. Remember the old Superman movies? We smoked tobacco. The dress code was not casual. There was a girl in my dorm from rural Tennessee. She wore sweatshirts and jeans, and it was worth remembering.

Now that I am back in school, I am paying for my books by selling t-shirts printed with LATE BLOOMER/BABY BOOMER. There is a picture of a lion cub. I draw heavily from preschool influences. An early childhood picture book called, *Leo the Late Bloomer*, a terrific story about a young lion's formative years, greatly influenced me and my decision to return to school. I have advice to give to the other Baby Boomers who return to college. We tend to talk a lot. Don't monopolize the classroom discussions. My next book, *When Putting Your Foot in Your Mouth is No Longer Possible: A Classroom Discussion Guide for Seniors*, will address this problem in more detail.

Older is wiser, anyone can be a Late Bloomer/Baby Boomer and return to school. Apply, register, do the process. Be proud, stand tall, order and wear your Late Bloomer/Baby Boomer t-shirt; (small & medium have been discontinued, large is on back order). A senior student, not to be confused with a graduating senior, does not have to worry about ruining their future. This is the future. So, go ahead, mess up, it is too late to ruin your life. You might even be surprised and earn an A.

About the Author

Patricia Finn was born and raised on Long Island, New York. Hoping to join the diplomatic corp. she attended American University in our Nation's Capitol. Plans change and she moved to Siesta Key, Florida, and became an ambassador for sand and sun. The mother of two, Patricia wrote for *Mothering* Magazine. She wrote and performed a weekly TV show for children which was aired on Sarasota's Channel 36. An active Storyteller at Florida schools and libraries, Patricia led workshops to promote early language development. Patricia's workshop "Beyond Mother Goose, the Reason for Rhyme" was presented at the National Center for Family Literacy's 2012 Annual Convention. A lover of children's books, she has written *Little Lion's Bedtime* and *Miguel Goes to School*. Patricia holds a Florida Department of Children and Families Director's Credential and has a License to Minister with United Christian Church. A lifelong learner, at the age of 61 she earned a degree from Southeastern University. According to Patricia, "I am living proof that you are never too old to do homework." *Walking with My Foot in My Mouth* is a collection of essays taken from FINNICKY, her blog for seniors. Visit Patricia at www.finnickyblog.com.

www.ingramcontent.com/pod-product-compliance
Lightning Source LLC
Chambersburg PA
CBHW021944290426
44108CB00012B/954